1 Kings 1–11, Proverbs & Ecclesiastes

The Rise and Fall of Solomon

John MacArthur

Thomas Nelson
Since 1798

MacArthur Bible Studies

1 Kings 1–11, Proverbs & Ecclesiastes: The Rise and Fall of Solomon

© 2016 by John MacArthur

Published in Nashville, Tennessee, by Nelson Books, an imprint of Thomas Nelson. Nelson Books and Thomas Nelson are registered trademarks of HarperCollins Christian Publishing, Inc.

Originally published in association with the literary agency of Wolgemuth & Associates, Inc. Original layout, design, and writing assistance by Gregory C. Benoit Publishing, Old Mystic, CT.

"Unleashing God's Truth, One Verse at a Time®" is a trademark of Grace to You. All rights reserved.

Thomas Nelson titles may be purchased in bulk for educational, business, fundraising, or sales promotional use. For information, please e-mail SpecialMarkets@ThomasNelson.com.

Some material from the Introduction, "Keys to the Text" and "Exploring the Meaning" sections taken from *The MacArthur Bible Commentary,* John MacArthur, Copyright © 2005 Thomas Nelson Publishers.

ISBN 978–07180–3475–7

First Printing January 2016 / Printed in the United States of America

HB 01.18.2024

CONTENTS

INTRODUCTION

David was one of Israel's greatest kings. During his reign, he unified the tribes of Israel, drove out invaders, conquered Jerusalem, and set the standard by which all kings that followed would be judged. He followed God all his days and was known as a man after the Lord's own heart. Yet David was also a great sinner. After ascending to the throne, he committed adultery with a woman named Bathsheba. Then, when he found out she was pregnant with his child, he conspired to have her husband, Uriah, killed in battle.

David soon made Bathsheba his wife, and she bore him a son. However, David's sinful acts displeased the Lord, and in time He sent Nathan the prophet to confront the king about what he had done. David admitted his guilt and was forgiven—but there were consequences. The child born of the unlawful union between David and Bathsheba soon became ill. David pleaded with God for seven days to spare the child's life, but in the end his son died.

After this, Bathsheba bore David a second son, whom God named Jedidiah, meaning "beloved of the Lord." David and Bathsheba named him Solomon. One might expect, given this family background, that he would not make a wise king. Yet Solomon became the wisest man who ever lived, and people from all over the world traveled to Jerusalem to learn from him. This demonstrates that wisdom is not based on one's upbringing or background or even resources. Wisdom is available to all people, regardless of their inherent skills or talents, because it is a gift from God.

In these twelve studies, we will examine the biblical events surrounding the rise and fall of Solomon as depicted in 1 Kings 1–11. We will also examine two books of biblical wisdom that Solomon (and others) wrote: Proverbs and Ecclesiastes. We will explore how true wisdom is not merely intellectual but also moral, how it gives us insight into the character of God, and how God gives His wisdom to anyone who asks. We will also look at how to speak with wisdom, act with wisdom, and persevere in wisdom. Through it all, we will learn some precious truths about the character of God, and we will see His great faithfulness in keeping His promises. We will learn, in short, what it means to be wise and walk by faith.

THE BOOK OF 1 KINGS

First and Second Kings were considered one book in the earliest Hebrew manuscripts. They were later divided into two books by the translators of the Greek version, known as the Septuagint. This division was later followed by the Latin Vulgate, English translations, and modern Hebrew Bibles. The earliest Hebrew manuscripts titled the one book *Kings*, after the first word in verse 1. The books of 1 and 2 Samuel and 1 and 2 Kings combined represent a chronicle of the entire history of Judah's and Israel's kingship from Saul to Zedekiah.

AUTHOR AND DATE

Jewish tradition proposed that Jeremiah wrote Kings. However, this is unlikely because Jeremiah never went to Babylon where the final event of the book takes place, and the date this event took place (561 BC) would have made him at least eighty-six years old at the time. Based on the fact 1 and 2 Kings emphasize the ministry of prophets, it seems likely it was written by an unnamed prophet who lived during the exile. The evidence seems to point to a single author living in Babylon who drew from pre-exilic source materials to complete the books.

The last narrated event in 2 Kings 25:27–30 sets the earliest possible date of completion, and because there is no record of the end of the Babylonian captivity in Kings, the Israelites' release from exile identifies the latest possible writing date. This sets the date for the works between 561–538 BC. This date is sometimes challenged on the basis of the "to this day" statements throughout the books, but it is best to understand these as coming from sources the author used rather than by the author himself.

BACKGROUND AND SETTING

The action in 1 and 2 Kings takes place in the whole land of Israel, from Dan to Beersheba, including the Transjordan. The author tells of four invading nations who played a dominant role in the affairs of Israel and Judah from 971 to 561 BC. The first was Egypt, who impacted Israel's history during the tenth century BC. The second was Syria (Aram), who posed a threat during the ninth century BC. The third was Assyria, who terrorized Palestine from the mid-eighth century to the late seventh century BC and ultimately destroyed the northern kingdom of Israel in 722 BC. The fourth was Babylon, who became the dominant power from 612 to 539 BC. The Babylonians destroyed Jerusalem in 586 BC, carrying the people of Judah into captivity.

The author of Kings, an exile in Babylon, wrote the book to communicate the lessons of Israel's history—from the ascension of Solomon in 971 BC to the destruction of Jerusalem in 586 BC—to the Jews living in exile. To accomplish this, he traced the histories of two sets of kings and two nations of disobedient people—Israel and Judah—to show how the people grew indifferent to God's law and His prophets. The sad reality he reveals is that all the kings of Israel and the majority of the kings of Judah were apostates who led their people into idolatry. Because of the kings' failure, God sent His prophets to confront the people with their sin. When this message was rejected, the people were ultimately carried into exile.

HISTORICAL AND THEOLOGICAL THEMES

The book of 1 Kings covers the events of Solomon's reign, followed by the divided kingdoms of Israel and Judah, and the eventual decline and fall of both kingdoms. Each king is introduced with (1) his name and relation to his predecessor, (2) his date of accession, (3) his age in coming to the throne (for kings of Judah only), (4) his length of reign, (5) his place of reign, (6) his mother's name (for Judah only), and (7) the author's spiritual appraisal of his reign. This introduction is followed by a narration of the events that occurred during the reign of each king. Each reign is concluded with (1) a citation of sources, (2) additional historical notes, (3) notice of death, (4) notice of burial, (5) the name of the successor, and (6) in a few instances, an added postscript.

Three theological themes are emphasized in Kings. The first is that the Lord judged Israel and Judah because of their disobedience to His law. This unfaithfulness on the part of the rebellious people was furthered by the apostasy of the evil kings who led them into idolatry, which caused the Lord to exercise His righteous wrath against them.

A second theme is that the word of the true prophets always came to pass. Several times we are led to understand the narrated events happened "according to the word of the LORD which He had spoken by His servants the prophets" (2 Kings 24:2; see also 1 Kings 13:2–3; 22:15–28; 2 Kings 23:16). The Lord always kept His Word, even His warnings of judgment.

A third theme is that the Lord remembered His promise to David (see 1 Kings 11:12; 15:4; 2 Kings 8:19). Even though the kings of the Davidic line proved to be disobedient, God did not bring David's family to an end. Even as the book closes, the line of David still exists, so there is hope for the coming "seed" of David (see 2 Samuel 7:12–16).

INTERPRETIVE CHALLENGES

The major interpretive challenge in 1 and 2 Kings concerns the *chronology of the kings of Israel and Judah*. Although the author provides abundant chronological data in the books, this information is difficult to interpret for two reasons. First, there seems to be inconsistencies in the information given. For instance, 1 Kings 16:23 states that Omri, king of Israel, began to reign in the thirty-first year of Asa, king of Judah, and that he reigned twelve years. However, according to 1 Kings 16:29, Omri was succeeded by his son Ahab in the thirty-eighth year of Asa, giving Omri a reign of only seven years, not twelve.

Second, extrabiblical sources (Greek, Assyrian, and Babylonian) seem to provide contrasting dates to those given in 1 and 2 Kings. For instance, Ahab and Jehu, kings of Israel, are believed to be mentioned in Assyrian records. Based on these records, Ahab's death can be fixed at 853 BC, and Jehu's reign at 841 BC. With these dates, it is possible to determine the date of the division of Israel from Judah was c. 931 BC, the fall of Samaria was 722 BC, and the fall of Jerusalem was 586 BC. However, when the total years of royal reigns in 1 and 2 Kings are added, the number for Israel is 241 years (not 210) and for Judah is 393 years (not 346).

The solution to this problem is to recognize there were some co-regencies in both kingdoms—a period when two kings ruled at the same time—so the overlapping years were counted twice in the total for both kings. Further, different methods of reckoning the years of a king's rule and even different calendars were used at differing times in the two kingdoms, resulting in the seeming internal inconsistencies. The accuracy of the chronology in Kings can be demonstrated and confirmed.

A second major interpretive challenge deals with Solomon's relationship to the Abrahamic and Davidic covenants. Some interpret 1 Kings 4:20–21 as the fulfillment of the promises given to Abraham (see Genesis 15:18–21; 22:17). However, according to Numbers 34:6, the western border of the land promised to Abraham was the Mediterranean Sea. Furthermore, in 1 Kings 5:1, Hiram is an independent king of Tyre and deals with Solomon as an equal. Solomon's empire was not the fulfillment of the land promise given to Abraham by the Lord, though a great portion of that land was under Solomon's control.

Further, Solomon's statements in 1 Kings 5:5 and 8:20 seem to represent his claims to be the promised seed of the Davidic covenant, and the author of Kings holds out the possibility that Solomon's temple was the fulfillment of the Lord's promise to David. However, it is equally clear that Solomon did not meet the conditions required for the fulfillment of the promise to David (see 11:9–13). In fact, none of the historical kings in the house of David met the conditions of complete obedience that was to be the sign of the Promised One. The books of Kings thus point Israel to a future hope under the Messiah when the covenants would be fulfilled.

THE BOOK OF PROVERBS

The book of Proverbs contains 513 of the more than 3,000 proverbs pondered by Solomon (see 1 Kings 4:32), along with proverbs from others whom Solomon might have influenced. The word *proverb* means "to be like"; thus, Proverbs is a book of comparisons between concrete images and life's most profound truths. These proverbs are simple moral statements (or illustrations) that highlight fundamental realities about life.

AUTHOR AND DATE

King Solomon, who ruled Israel from 971–931 BC, most likely authored the didactic section (Proverbs 1–9) and the wisdom of 10:1–22:16. However, he is likely only the compiler of the "sayings of the wise" in 22:17–24:34, which are of an uncertain date before Solomon's reign. The sayings in Proverbs 25–29 were originally composed by Solomon but copied and included later by Judah's King

Hezekiah (c. 715–686 BC). Proverbs 30 reflects the words of Agur and Proverbs 31 the words of Lemuel, who perhaps was Solomon.

BACKGROUND AND SETTING

In Proverbs, Solomon the sage gives insight into the "knotty" issues of life that were not directly addressed in the Old Testament books of the Law or the Prophets. Though practical, Proverbs is not superficial because it contains moral and ethical elements that emphasize an upright living that flows out of a right relationship with God. Proverbs is both a pattern for the tender impartation of truth from generation to generation as well as a vast resource for the content of the truth to be taught. It contains the principles and applications of Scripture that the godly characters of the Bible illustrate in their lives.

HISTORICAL AND THEOLOGICAL THEMES

Solomon came to the throne with great promise, privilege, and opportunity. God had granted his request for understanding, and his wisdom exceeded all others (see 1 Kings 3:9–12; 4:29–31). However, the shocking reality is that Solomon failed to live out the truth he knew and had even taught to his son Rehoboam, who subsequently rejected his father's teaching.

The two major themes that are interwoven and overlap throughout Proverbs are wisdom and folly. Wisdom—which includes knowledge, understanding, instruction, discretion, and obedience—is built on the fear of the Lord and the Word of God. The recurring promise of Proverbs is that, generally speaking, the wise (the righteous who obey God) live longer, prosper, and experience joy and the goodness of God.

Folly is everything opposite of wisdom, and the promise of Proverbs is that the fool, generally speaking, suffers shame and death. However, it must be remembered that this general promise is balanced by the reality that the wicked sometimes prosper, though only temporarily. The book of Job illustrates there are occasions when the godly wise are struck with disaster and suffering.

INTERPRETIVE CHALLENGES

A major challenge of Proverbs is the elusive nature of wisdom literature itself. Much like Jesus' parables in the New Testament, the intended truths of the proverbs are often veiled from understanding if given only a cursory glance, and thus must be pondered in the heart. A second challenge is the extensive use of parallelism in Proverbs, which is placing truths side by side so the second line expands, completes, defines, emphasizes, or reaches the logical conclusion—and, in some cases, the contrasting point of view. Often, the actual parallel is only implied.

Another challenge involves the contexts in which the proverbs were spoken. This includes the *setting of the proverb* (largely the context of a young man in the royal court of the king). It also includes the *setting of the book* as a whole, understanding that its teachings are to be understood in light of the rest of Scripture. There is also the *historical context*, in which the principles and truths draw on illustrations from their own day.

A final challenge comes in understanding that proverbs are divine guidelines and wise observations, but not inflexible laws or absolute promises. These expressions of general truth usually have "exceptions" due to the uncertainty of life and unpredictable behavior of fallen men. God does not guarantee a uniform outcome for each proverb; but in studying them and applying them, one comes to contemplate the mind of God, His character, His attributes, His works, and His blessings.

The Book of Ecclesiastes

The English title *Ecclesiastes* comes from the Greek term *ekklesiastes*, which means "preacher." Both the Greek and Latin versions derive their titles from the Hebrew title *Qoheleth*, which means "one who calls or gathers" the people. Along with Ruth, Song of Solomon, Esther, and Lamentations, Ecclesiastes stands with the Old Testament books of the Megilloth, or "five scrolls." Later rabbis read these books in the synagogue on five special occasions during the year—Ecclesiastes being read on Pentecost.

Author and Date

The autobiographical profile of the book's writer unmistakably points to Solomon. The titles used fit Solomon, "son of David, king in Jerusalem"; the author's moral odyssey chronicles Solomon's life; and the role of one who "taught the people knowledge" and wrote "many proverbs" (12:9) corresponds to his accomplishments. Solomon likely wrote the book in his later years (no later than c. 931 BC) to warn the young people of his kingdom to avoid walking through life on the path of human wisdom.

BACKGROUND AND SETTING

After Solomon received a "wise and understanding heart" from the Lord (1 Kings 3:7–12), he gained renown for rendering insightful decisions and developed a reputation that attracted "all the kings of the earth" to his courts (4:34). In addition, he composed songs and proverbs, an activity befitting only the ablest of sages. Solomon's wisdom, like Job's wealth, surpassed the wisdom "of all the men of the East" (4:30). Ecclesiastes is applicable to all who benefit from the principles Solomon drew on his life experiences. Solomon's aim was to answer some of life's most challenging questions, particularly when they seemed contrary to his expectations. This has led some people, unwisely, to take the view that Ecclesiastes is a book of skepticism.

HISTORICAL AND THEOLOGICAL THEMES

Ecclesiastes represents the painful autobiography of Solomon, who, for much of his life, squandered God's blessings on his own personal pleasure. He wrote the book to warn subsequent generations not to make the same tragic error. Solomon uses the Hebrew word translated *vanity, vanities,* or *vain life* thirty-eight times to express the futile attempt to be satisfied in this life apart from God.

The wise king gave a considerable portion of the book to addressing the dilemma of what profit a person gains from his labors on earth. The impossibility of knowing the inner workings of God's creation and the personal providence of God were also deeply troubling to the king. However, the reality of judgment for all, despite many unknowns, emerged as the great certainty. In light of this judgment by God, the only fulfilled life is one lived in proper recognition of God and service to Him. Any other kind of life is frustrating and pointless.

The tragic results of Solomon's personal experience, coupled with the insights of his extraordinary wisdom, make Ecclesiastes a book from which all believers can be warned but also grow in their faith. The book shows that if a person perceives each day of existence, labor, and basic provision as a gift from

God, that person will live an abundant life. However, those who look to be satisfied apart from God will live with futility, regardless of their accumulations.

INTERPRETIVE CHALLENGES

The word translated *vanity* is used in at least three ways throughout the book. In each case, it looks at the nature of man's activity as *fleeting*, which has in view the vapor-like or transitory nature of life; *futile*, which focuses on the cursed condition of the universe and the debilitating effects it has on man's experience; or *incomprehensible*, which gives consideration to life's unanswerable questions. Solomon draws on all three meanings.

Although the context in each case determines which meaning Solomon employs, the most recurring meaning is *incomprehensible*, referring to the mysteries of God's purposes. Solomon's conclusion to "fear God and keep His commandments" (12:13) is more than the book's summary; it is the only hope of the good life and the only reasonable response of faith and obedience to our sovereign God. The Lord works out all activities under the sun, each in its time according to His perfect plan, but He also discloses only as much as His perfect wisdom dictates—and then holds all people accountable. Those who refuse to take God and His Word seriously are doomed to lives of the severest vanity.

1

THE RISE OF SOLOMON

1 Kings 2:1–3:28

DRAWING NEAR

What are some of the benefits of making compromises? Under what circumstances would you refuse to compromise?

_____

_____

_____

THE CONTEXT

The book of 1 Kings begins with the final years of David's reign. By this time David is seventy years of age, and circulatory problems have plagued him to the point that he has trouble keeping warm. So his servants propose a solution in keeping with the medical practices of the day. They find a beautiful young woman named Abishag to watch over him at night and warm him with her body heat. In this manner Abishag joins David's harem, though the text makes it clear that she remained a virgin.

The news of David's failing health soon prompted Adonijah, David's fourth son, to assert his claim to the throne. By this point Adonijah's older brothers Amnon and Absalom (and evidently Chileab) were dead, making him the heir apparent. Like Absalom, Adonijah was an attractive young man, and his ambition led him to raise a small army to support his claim. He soon gained the support of Joab, David's powerful general, and the high priest Abiathar.

However, the prophet Nathan knew Adonijah was not God's choice for the next king. That distinction would fall to Solomon—the second child born to David and Bathsheba. Nathan's intervention prompted David to formally recognize Solomon as his successor, even though he was not next in line for the kingship. Adonijah's support eroded, and he begged Solomon for mercy. Solomon spared his life, provided he proved "himself a worthy man" (1 Kings 1:52) and did not seek to reclaim the throne.

Once the succession was secure, Solomon began his reign on a good footing. He asked God to give him wisdom to shepherd His people, and the Lord answered by giving him not only wisdom but also great riches and power. Solomon's kingdom would grow to be one of the most powerful in the world at the time. Unfortunately, in the process Solomon would allow a number of compromises to creep in that would ultimately set him up for disaster.

Keys to the Text

Read 1 Kings 2:1–3:28, noting the key words and phrases indicated below.

David's Final Instructions: As the time of David's life on earth draws to a close, he summons Solomon, his chosen heir, to impart some final wisdom and instructions to him.

2:1. HE CHARGED SOLOMON: Leaders typically gave final instructions to their successors when they were handing over power to them (see Deuteronomy 31:7–8; Joshua 23:1–16; 1 Samuel 12:1–25). David followed this practice by giving Solomon a final exhortation.

2. BE STRONG, THEREFORE, AND PROVE YOURSELF A MAN: David told Solomon he would be going "the way of all the earth" and that Solomon needed to be strong. In this way David sought to encourage and prepare Solomon for the difficult tasks that lay ahead.

3. KEEP THE CHARGE OF THE LORD YOUR GOD: David admonished Solomon to obey the Mosaic Law so he could have a successful kingship. God

had made an unconditional covenant with him in 2 Samuel 7:4–17, and He would confirm that covenant to Solomon (see 1 Kings 9:5). In this way, the Lord promised the perpetuation of the Davidic dynasty over Israel.

4. IF YOUR SONS TAKE HEED TO THEIR WAY: The king's obedience to the Law was a necessary condition for the fulfillment of the divine promise. Unfortunately, none of David's descendants would remain faithful to God's Law, and none of them would meet the conditions for the fulfillment of the promise.

> REWARD AND PUNISHMENT: *David not only encourages Solomon to be courageous and faithful to the Lord but also charges him with tying up some loose ends from his reign.*

5. YOU KNOW ALSO WHAT JOAB THE SON OF ZERUIAH DID TO ME: David concluded his instructions by commanding Solomon to reward one man who had been faithful to him and to punish two men who had wronged him. One of those men whom Solomon was to punish was David's former general. Joab's zeal had led him to murder two men—Abner and Amasa—after warfare had ceased, which under the Law made him a murderer (see Deuteronomy 19:11–13). Joab had also gone against David's direct orders to not kill his son Absalom.

7. SHOW KINDNESS TO THE SONS OF BARZILLAI: The man whom David wanted to reward was Barzillai, who had brought supplies to him and his troops when they fled from Jerusalem (see 2 Samuel 17:27–29). David instructed Solomon to repay this kindness by showing similar kindness to Barzillai's sons. Allowing them to eat at Solomon's table represented a position of honor that could also include a royal stipend.

8. SHIMEI THE SON OF GERA: Shimei had cursed David and thrown stones at him as he was escaping from Absalom, which were actions worthy of death (see 2 Samuel 16:5–13). David had spared his life at the time, not wanting further bloodshed, but he now counseled Solomon through subtle means to arrange for his just punishment.

11. DAVID REIGNED OVER ISRAEL . . . FORTY YEARS: David ruled from approximately 1011 BC to 971 BC, probably with Solomon as co-regent during his final year.

3

BROTHERLY TREACHERY: Solomon's rivals move in after the death of King David to lay their claim to the throne. One of these contenders draws Solomon's mother into his treachery.

12. HIS KINGDOM WAS FIRMLY ESTABLISHED: Solomon enjoyed the Lord's approval for his succession, but not everyone had agreed with God's choice.

15. ALL ISRAEL HAD SET THEIR EXPECTATIONS ON ME: As the direct heir to the throne, Adonijah might have been correct in his claim that "all Israel" expected him to be king. However, as the Lord would say through the prophet Isaiah, "My thoughts are not your thoughts, nor are your ways My ways" (55:8). He had already chosen Solomon to be the next ruler.

17. GIVE ME ABISHAG: Adonijah went to Bathsheba, Solomon's mother, and asked her to persuade Solomon to give him Abishag as his wife. In the ancient Near East, possession of the royal harem was a sign of kingship, so Adonijah's request was an attempt to support his claim and perhaps generate a revolt. Bathsheba didn't see through the treachery.

22. ASK FOR HIM THE KINGDOM ALSO: Solomon immediately recognized Adonijah's request as the prelude to his usurping of the throne. Adonijah's request violated the terms of loyalty Solomon had previously specified, so he pronounced a legal death sentence on him.

26. GO TO ANATHOTH: This was a priestly town located three miles northeast of Jerusalem. It was there that Abiathar, the disloyal high priest who had previously supported Adonijah as king, lived in banishment.

27. FULFILL THE WORD OF THE LORD: Solomon's removal of Abiathar from the office of priest fulfilled God's prophecy in 1 Samuel 2:30–35 that Eli's line of priests would be cut off. The subsequent appointment of Zadok for this position reestablished the line of Eleazar/Phinehas as God had promised (see Numbers 25:10–13).

THE END OF JOAB AND SHIMEI: After dealing with the treachery of Adonijah, Solomon fulfills his father's last wishes to punish Joab and Shimei for their deeds.

28. JOAB FLED TO THE TABERNACLE: For years Joab had served David as commander of his army, but after the king's death he defected from God's choice and supported Adonijah. When Joab heard Adonijah had been put to

death, he fled to the tabernacle and took hold of the altar. Joab knew he would have been killed already if he had not been so popular with the army.

31. STRIKE HIM DOWN: The Law of Moses offered protection at the altar for those guilty of accidental crimes, but not premeditated murder (see Exodus 21:12–14). For this reason, Solomon ordered Benaiah to administer the violent death sought by David.

34. HE WAS BURIED ... IN THE WILDERNESS: The tomb of Joab's father was near Bethlehem. Joab's house was probably on the edge of the Judean wilderness, east of Bethlehem.

36. DO NOT GO OUT: Shimei had not provoked Solomon as directly as Adonijah had, so Solomon kept him under close watch by confining him to Jerusalem. Shimei agreed to remain in Jerusalem, but when two of his slaves escaped, he went in search of them.

40. WENT TO ACHISH AT GATH: Achish was the ruler of Gath, a major Philistine city about thirty miles southwest of Jerusalem. Shimei ultimately found his slaves there, but word reached Solomon that he had broken his order. It would prove to be the last mistake Shimei ever made.

45. THE THRONE OF DAVID SHALL BE ESTABLISHED: In contrast to Shimei's curse against David in 2 Samuel 16:5–8, the Lord's blessing was to come through the ruler of David's line, not through Saul's line. With the death of Shimei, all the rival factions were eliminated.

THE REIGN OF SOLOMON: Now that the succession has been settled, Solomon begins to make political alliances to secure the land for the Israelites.

3:1. SOLOMON MADE A TREATY WITH PHARAOH: This pharaoh was probably Siamun, the next-to-last ruler of the twenty-first dynasty. Solomon's alliance with him demonstrated how powerful Israel was becoming, as the Egyptians did not ordinarily make such agreements.

AND MARRIED PHARAOH'S DAUGHTER: Pharaoh's daughter would be the most politically significant of Solomon's 700 wives. However, the Lord had expressly forbidden His people to intermarry with the pagan nations, warning them such marriages would lead the people astray.

2. SACRIFICED AT THE HIGH PLACES: The Canaanites worshiped their gods on hilltops, frequently in open-air shrines. The Israelites were commanded

to destroy these altars, and after the temple was completed, God's people were forbidden to use the sites at all. But they didn't listen, and their disobedience eventually led Israel into *syncretism*, the act of combining pagan practices with God's ordained worship.

NO HOUSE BUILT FOR THE NAME OF THE LORD: In the ancient Near East, to identify a temple with a god's name meant the god owned the place and dwelt there. God had promised to choose one place "to put His name for His dwelling place" (Deuteronomy 12:5), and the temple at Jerusalem was to be that place.

A BLANK CHECK: The Lord appears to Solomon in a dream and offers to give him anything he desires. Solomon's request to the Lord is surprising.

3. SOLOMON LOVED THE LORD: Solomon began well. He loved the Lord and followed his father's example of walking according to God's Word. He sincerely desired to be faithful to the Lord and be a good king, as David had been for most of his reign.

EXCEPT THAT HE SACRIFICED: This dangerous word *except* alerts us to Solomon's area of weakness. These "high places," even if they were now dedicated to the Lord, were likely former sites of Baal worship. At the least, they were an example of God's people imitating the ways of the world, worshiping Him at places of convenience rather than in the tabernacle.

4. THE KING WENT TO GIBEON: A town about seven miles northwest of Jerusalem, where the tabernacle of Moses and the original bronze altar were located.

5. THE LORD APPEARED TO SOLOMON IN A DREAM: God often gave revelation in dreams, but this dream was unique because it was a two-way conversation between Him and Solomon. The Lord permitted Solomon to ask for anything he desired, and in so doing tested Solomon's heart to discover his priorities. In spite of David's adultery, he had been a man after God's own heart. Solomon now had the opportunity to show he would follow his father's footsteps.

6. GREAT MERCY . . . GREAT KINDNESS: These terms imply covenant faithfulness. Solomon viewed his succession to David as evidence of the Lord's faithfulness to His promises to David.

7. I AM A LITTLE CHILD: Solomon was probably twenty years old when he assumed the throne. His answer to the Lord demonstrated a wholesome humility, as he recognized it was a huge responsibility to lead God's people. At this point, he acknowledged his own limitations and understood he could not shepherd Israel under his own power. He needed God's help.

8. IN THE MIDST OF YOUR PEOPLE: Solomon underscored the fact that Israel was the Lord's nation, not his own, and that he was accountable to God for the welfare of His people. Based on the census in 2 Samuel 24:9, which recorded 800,000 men of fighting age in Israel and 500,000 in Judah, the total population at this time was more than four million people.

9. AN UNDERSTANDING HEART: The Hebrew word translated *understanding* means "to hear, listen to, obey." Solomon wisely asked the Lord to give him an obedient heart that was turned fully toward the Word of God.

A GOOD CHOICE: Solomon's request pleases the Lord, and He grants wisdom in abundance—along with things that Solomon didn't ask for.

10. THE SPEECH PLEASED THE LORD: God was delighted Solomon had not asked for personal benefits (long life or riches) or the death of his enemies. Christians would do well to imitate Solomon's example, asking God to give them a hunger to understand and obey His Word. A heart for God is a gift and not something that a person can attain by sheer willpower. But today, we have the presence of the Holy Spirit in our lives, and He is eager to give us this very thing.

11. LONG LIFE . . . RICHES . . . THE LIFE OF YOUR ENEMIES: Requests such as these are more typical of what a person might ask if given such *carte blanche* by the Lord—yet these things reflect the wisdom of the world, not the wisdom of God.

12. THERE HAS NOT BEEN ANYONE LIKE YOU: God gave Solomon a unique type of wisdom and insight. This great understanding would enable him to write the bulk of what is known as the Wisdom Literature, including the books of Proverbs, Ecclesiastes, and the Song of Solomon.

13. I HAVE ALSO GIVEN YOU WHAT YOU HAVE NOT ASKED: Solomon asked for wisdom and understanding, and the Lord granted his request in superabundance. This is the way God loves to give to His people. As James

reminds us, "If any of you lacks wisdom, let him ask of God, who gives to all liberally and without reproach, and it will be given to him" (1:5).

14. IF YOU WALK IN MY WAYS: God's gift of wisdom to Solomon was conditional, but He placed stipulations on His offer of long life. Unfortunately, Solomon would not meet those conditions and would die before reaching seventy—a relatively young age in Solomon's day.

WISDOM IN PRACTICE: Two prostitutes come to Solomon with a difficult case. There are no witnesses, and it will require great wisdom to discern the truth.

16. HARLOTS CAME TO THE KING: It seems surprising that two prostitutes would stand before the greatest king of the age and plead their private cases, but this shows how wisely Solomon ruled. In Israel, the king was the ultimate "judge" of the land, and Solomon made himself available to all types of people within his kingdom. His wisdom and justice were accessible to all.

23. THE ONE SAYS . . . AND THE OTHER SAYS: The difficulty of this case was there were no witnesses to corroborate one woman's story over the other. It was a matter of choosing which one to believe, and neither prostitute would have been considered a reliable witness.

25. DIVIDE THE LIVING CHILD IN TWO: Solomon bypassed the conflicting claims of the women and searched their hearts for the truth. In ordering his servants to cut the child in two, Solomon knew the liar would not object, while the real mother would never permit such a horrible fate.

28. FEARED THE KING: Israel was in awe of Solomon and willing to submit to his rule because of his wisdom from God.

UNLEASHING THE TEXT

1) What were David's final instructions to Solomon? How did the actions of Joab and Shimei lead to Solomon fulfilling these instructions and putting the two men to death?

_____

_____

_____

2) Why did Joab flee to the tabernacle and grab hold of the altar? Why was no protection afforded to him there?

_____

_____

_____

3) Why did Solomon ask for wisdom instead of power or wealth or freedom from his enemies? Why did God grant his request so generously?

_____

_____

_____

4) If you had been in Solomon's place, how would you have dealt with the two prostitutes? How did Solomon's judgment demonstrate wisdom?

_____

_____

_____

EXPLORING THE MEANING

Wisdom is moral, not merely intellectual. When the Bible speaks of wisdom, it is not talking about a person's intelligence. From God's perspective, wisdom is a moral quality. A wise person lives life skillfully because he has discernment and can distinguish between good and evil. A person can be a mathematical genius or a scholar and still be considered a fool if he does not understand the truths of Scripture. A person can be a smart fool but not a wise atheist.

Wisdom has nothing to do with a person's inherent natural gifts. It is not gained through a good education, nor is it made more available to certain social classes or income brackets. Wisdom comes only from God, and it is a gift He gives to those who ask for it. Solomon described wisdom and understanding as "more precious than rubies" (Proverbs 3:15). Nothing we desire can ever compare with wisdom, "for her proceeds are better than the profits of silver" (verse 14). Wisdom can bring long life, riches, and great honor, and it enables a person to live a peaceable and pleasant life (see verses 16–17).

The Word of God contains the words of life, and they are a treasure beyond anything the world has to offer. As David wrote, "The law of the LORD is perfect . . . more to be desired . . . than much fine gold; sweeter also than honey and the honeycomb. Moreover by them Your servant is warned, and in keeping them there is great reward" (Psalm 19:7, 10–11).

Wisdom comes through God's Word, and He gives it freely to those who ask. Wisdom is seen in having the mind of Christ (see 1 Corinthians 2:16). When a person is wise, he sees a situation as Christ would see it. This wisdom, of course, only comes through God's Word, and God Himself has promised to give understanding to anyone who will ask for it.

This does not mean a person is uninvolved in gaining wisdom. It is an active skill, and one that requires practice to grow and mature. But wisdom is available to anyone who desires it—and it is a free gift. What's more, it is a gift that God is eager to bestow on all His children, and He's always ready to give more whenever we ask. As James tells us, "If any of you lacks wisdom, let him ask of God, who gives to all liberally and without reproach, and it will be given to him" (James 1:5).

Solomon asked the Lord for wisdom, and God gave it to him in abundance. Today, God's wisdom does not come in the form of a dream but through the gospel. In 1 Corinthians 1:24, Paul calls Christ "the wisdom of God," and in Colossians 3:16, he says that this wisdom is gained through the study of "the word of Christ." God is eager to bestow wisdom on us, and that wisdom is found in the pages of Scripture.

The more we obey God's Word, the deeper our love grows for Him. As a young man, Solomon loved the Lord deeply and wanted to be obedient to His Word. In this, he was like his father, David, who made it a lifelong priority to follow God's law. Unfortunately, Solomon laid a trap for himself early in his kingship by mixing pagan practices into his worship and sacrificing to the Lord on the hilltops where the Canaanites had formerly worshiped the false god Baal.

During the course of his lifetime, Solomon's love for the Lord would grow lukewarm. In contrast, David's love for God grew stronger and deeper the longer he walked in obedience. The difference is that David repented of his sinful behaviors, while Solomon continued to excuse them. For all his wisdom, Solomon would not prove to be faithful to God.

When we obey God, we give Him the opportunity to demonstrate His faithfulness, power, and love in our lives. We gain a deeper understanding of His character as we walk in obedience, and this leads us to have a deeper love for Him. However, the opposite is also true: if we persist in ignoring His Word, our hearts will grow cold toward God.

REFLECTING ON THE TEXT

5) How would you define *wisdom* and *understanding* in your own words? Give some practical examples of each.

_____

_____

_____

_____

6) Why was God pleased with Solomon's request? Why did He give him so many other things as well? What does this suggest about the relationship between wisdom and riches?

_____

_____

_____

7) In what ways are wisdom and understanding more valuable to a person than anything else the world has to offer?

_____

_____

_____

8) What role does obedience play in gaining wisdom? How are wisdom and obedience inseparably linked?

_____

_____

_____

PERSONAL RESPONSE

9) In what areas of your life do you require wisdom at present? Take time right now to ask the Lord to give you wisdom in addressing those issues.

_____

_____

_____

10) What things are most important to you? What are you striving for most actively—success, wealth, wisdom, or understanding?

_____

_____

_____

2

BUILDING THE TEMPLE
1 Kings 6:1–38; 8:1–9:9

DRAWING NEAR

What was the most ambitious project you ever set out to do? What was
the result?

_____

_____

_____

THE CONTEXT

Solomon began his reign armed with God's wisdom and His blessings for
wealth and honor. As he set up his government, he was careful to choose
men who were loyal to him and who had served his father, David, faithfully
during his reign. Solomon also chose men who were skilled in areas necessary to the functioning of a strong government, including priests, record
keepers, and administrators. The man Solomon selected to lead his military
was Benaiah, who had followed his order to strike down Joab. Adoniram,
whom Solomon put in charge of the labor force, had also served under David
(see 2 Samuel 20:24).

Solomon appointed twelve district governors and assigned each a month of the year to supply the kings' household with provisions and food. Solomon did not appoint these governors following the traditional tribal lines of Israel, as it would have made it difficult for some areas to support the economic demands during their month of provision. While this may have been a wise economic decision at the time, it likely contributed to problems that would ultimately lead to the breakdown of the kingdom after Solomon's death.

The reign of Solomon ushered in a time of peace and prosperity for Israel, and its borders now encompassed the lands God had promised to Abraham (see Genesis 15:18–21). "Judah and Israel were as numerous as the sand on the seashore; they ate, they drank and they were happy" (1 Kings 4:20). The stage was set for Solomon to begin the task of building the temple "for the Name of the LORD" (1 Kings 5:5), and to do so he called on an old ally of his father, Hiram the king of Tyre, to obtain the necessary lumber for the construction.

The temple would serve to remind the king and his people of the serious state of their sin and God's forgiveness and grace. It was to be the center of their worship of the one true God and a place of prayer and reading His Word. Along with the activities of worship, the very structure of the temple was intended to prepare the people to recognize the true Lamb of God, Jesus Christ, who would take away the sin of the world.

KEYS TO THE TEXT

Read 1 Kings 6:1–38, noting the key words and phrases indicated below.

> *LAYING THE FOUNDATION: Now that the land of Israel is at peace, Solomon begins work on the project his father was not allowed to undertake: building the temple.*

6:1. FOUR HUNDRED AND EIGHTIETH YEAR: Solomon laid the foundation of the temple 480 years after the exodus from Egypt. The 480 years are to be taken as the actual years between the exodus and the building of the temple, because references to numbers of years in the books of 1 and 2 Kings are consistently taken in a literal fashion.

FOURTH YEAR: These events took place in 966 BC, which means the Israelites' exodus from Egypt can be dated to approximately 1445 BC.

2. ITS LENGTH WAS SIXTY CUBITS: Normally, a cubit was about 18 inches. This would make the temple structure 90 feet long, 30 feet wide, and 45 feet high. However, 2 Chronicles 3:3 may indicate the longer royal cubit of approximately 21 inches was used in the construction of the temple. Based on this measurement, the temple structure would have been 105 feet long, 35 feet wide, and 52 feet high.

3. THE VESTIBULE IN FRONT ON THE SANCTUARY: This vestibule was a porch about fifteen feet long in front of the temple building proper.

4. WINDOWS WITH BEVELED FRAMES: These openings high on the inner side of the temple wall had lattices or shutters that could be opened, shut, or partially opened. They served to let out the vapors of the lamps and the smoke of incense as well as to give light.

5. HE BUILT CHAMBERS: Another attached structure surrounded the main building, excluding the vestibule. It provided rooms off the main hall to house temple personnel and store equipment and treasure.

6. LOWEST CHAMBER . . . MIDDLE . . . THIRD: The structure in which the chambers were built was three stories high. Each upper story was one cubit wider than the one below it. The beams supporting the stories were not inserted into the temple walls but rested on recessed ledges.

7. STONE FINISHED AT THE QUARRY: Solomon constructed the temple using precut and prefitted materials that had been moved on rollers to the site. The relative quiet of this process would have been consistent with the sacredness of the undertaking.

8. DOORWAY FOR THE MIDDLE STORY: The entrance to the side rooms of the temple was on the south side, probably in the middle. Access to the second and third stories was made by means of a spiral staircase that led through the middle story to the third floor.

A GENTLE REMINDER: As Solomon is building the temple, the Lord speaks to him and reiterates that the fulfillment of His word to David is contingent on Solomon's obedience.

11. THE WORD OF THE LORD CAME TO SOLOMON: The Lord likely spoke to Solomon this time through a prophet. God's words echoed David's prior challenge to his son to walk in God's ways and "keep His statutes, His commandments, His judgments, and His testimonies . . . that the LORD may fulfill His word which He spoke concerning me" (1 Kings 2:3–4).

13. I WILL DWELL AMONG THE CHILDREN OF ISRAEL: Previously, God had said to His people, "I will dwell among the children of Israel and be their God" (Exodus 29:45). The use of the same words here implied that Solomon's temple was the legitimate successor to the tabernacle. However, the Lord warned Solomon and Israel that only their continued obedience—and not the temple—would guarantee His continued presence.

THE SPLENDOR OF THE TEMPLE: Solomon spares no expense in building and furnishing the temple to the Lord. He has much of the interior of the structure overlaid with pure gold.

16. THE MOST HOLY PLACE: This inner sanctuary, partitioned off from the main hall by cedar planks, was a perfect cube about thirty feet on each side. It was the most sacred area of the temple. The tabernacle also had a "Most Holy" place (Exodus 26:33–34).

17. THE TEMPLE SANCTUARY: This was the Holy Place, just outside the Most Holy Place, and was 60 feet long, 30 feet wide, and 45 feet high. It housed the altar of incense, the golden tables of the showbread, and the golden lampstands.

19. THE ARK OF THE COVENANT OF THE LORD: The ark was a rectangular box made of acacia wood that had been constructed by the craftsman Bezalel when the Israelites were camped at Mount Sinai. It served as the receptacle for the two tablets of the Ten Commandments and the place in the Most Holy Place where the presence of the Lord met Israel.

20. OVERLAID IT WITH PURE GOLD: Solomon had the workers beat gold into fine sheets and then hammer it to fit over the beautifully embellished wood. The workers then attached the gold to every surface in the temple proper, both in the Holy Place and in the Most Holy Place, so that no wood or stone was visible.

23. TWO CHERUBIM OF OLIVE WOOD: These sculptured winged creatures, with human faces overlaid with gold, represented angelic beings who were guardians of God's presence. They were fifteen feet tall and fifteen feet between wing tips and were placed on either side of the ark.

29. PALM TREES: This image was reminiscent of the Garden of Eden. The palm tree represented "tree of life . . . in the midst of the garden" (Genesis 2:9).

All of the details in the temple signified the magnificence of God's nature and His uncommon glory.

31. DOORS OF OLIVE WOOD: Magnificent doors separated the inner court of the temple and the Holy Place, as well as the Holy Place and the Most Holy Place.

36. THE INNER COURT: This walled-in space that surrounded the temple was also called "the court of the priests" or the "upper court." The alternation of timber beams in the wall with masonry was common in Mediterranean construction.

38. SEVEN YEARS: From foundation to finishing, it took Solomon seven years and six months to build the temple. It was completed in Solomon's eleventh year of rule (959 BC), in the eighth month.

Read 1 Kings 8:1–9:9, noting the key words and phrases indicated below.

THE ARK ARRIVES: The time finally arrives for the dedication of the temple. As the ark is brought into the Most Holy Place, the cloud of God's presence descends and fills the place.

8:1. THE ELDERS OF ISRAEL AND ALL THE HEADS OF THE TRIBES: The elders of Israel were respected men in charge of local government and justice who advised the king on important matters of state.

2. THE SEVENTH MONTH: Solomon finished building the temple in the eighth month of the previous year. This celebration, then, did not take place until eleven months later. Apparently, Solomon scheduled the dedication of the temple to coincide with the Feast of Tabernacles held in the seventh month, when there would be a general assembly of the people in Jerusalem. That was also a Jubilee year, so it was especially appropriate.

6. THEY BROUGHT UP THE ARK: The priests and Levites transported the ark of the covenant from the tent that David had made for it in Jerusalem (see 2 Samuel 6:17). They also brought to the temple the tabernacle and all its furnishings, which had been located at Gibeon.

8. THE POLES EXTENDED: God had originally commanded that poles be used to carry the ark. These poles were left protruding so the high priest could use them as a guide when he entered the dark inner sanctuary.

9. TWO TABLETS OF STONE: At this time, the ark of the covenant contained only the two tablets inscribed with the Ten Commandments. It no longer contained the pot of manna (see Exodus 16:33) and Aaron's rod that budded (see Numbers 17:10).

10. THE CLOUD FILLED THE HOUSE OF THE LORD: The cloud was the glory of the Lord—the visible symbol of His presence—and it signaled the Lord's approval of this new temple. A similar manifestation took place when the tabernacle was dedicated (see Exodus 40:34–35).

SOLOMON'S DEDICATION: Solomon gives a speech to the people in which he states he had become the fulfillment of God's promise to David. Unfortunately, his claim is premature.

12. HE WOULD DWELL IN THE DARK CLOUD: Solomon addressed this solemn declaration to the Lord. He recognized this darkness was the manifestation of the Lord's presence among His people and affirmed he had built the temple so the Lord could dwell there.

14. THEN THE KING TURNED: Solomon turned around from addressing the Lord and spoke to the assembly of Israel gathered at the temple.

20. THE LORD HAS FULFILLED HIS WORD: Solomon began by relating the story of 2 Samuel 7:12–16 and claimed that he, having built the temple, had become the fulfillment of God's promise to his father. Later, God would appear to Solomon and declare the necessity of obedience for the establishment of Solomon's throne.

22. SOLOMON STOOD BEFORE THE ALTAR: Solomon moved to the altar of burnt offering and offered a prayer of consecration. In this prayer, he affirmed no god could compare to Israel's God, asked the Lord for His continued presence and protection, and listed seven typical Israelite prayers that would require the Lord's response. These supplications recalled the detailed list of curses ascribed in Deuteronomy 28:15–68 for the breaking of the Law.

27. HEAVEN . . . CANNOT CONTAIN YOU: Solomon confessed that though the Lord had chosen to dwell among His people, He far transcended containment by anything in creation.

31. WHEN ANYONE SINS AGAINST HIS NEIGHBOR: Solomon's requests included prayers that the Lord would judge between the wicked and the righteous; forgive sins that had caused defeat in battle, drought, and national

calamities; show mercy to God-fearing foreigners; give victory in battle; and bring restoration after captivity.

BLESSING AND SACRIFICE: Solomon concludes the dedication ceremony by blessing the assembly and offering the first sacrifices in the temple to the Lord.

54. HE AROSE FROM BEFORE THE ALTAR: Solomon's benediction was a brief recapitulation of the preceding prayer, in which he affirmed the faithfulness of the Lord to the people and exhorted the people to remain faithful to the Lord.

62. OFFERED SACRIFICES BEFORE THE LORD: To complete the dedication, Solomon led the people in presenting peace offerings to the Lord, during which they consumed 22,000 bulls and 120,000 sheep and goats. Although the number of sacrifices offered seems high, it was in keeping with the magnitude of this event.

64. THERE HE OFFERED BURNT OFFERINGS: The bronze altar could not accommodate such a number of sacrifices, so Solomon consecrated the middle courtyard and then likely set up a series of auxiliary altars there.

GOD'S SECOND APPEARANCE: God again appears to Solomon to tell the king his prayers have been heard. But this visit comes with a stern warning.

9:1. WHEN SOLOMON HAD FINISHED: God did not appear to Solomon this second time until he had completed the building of his own palace in 946 BC (see 1 Kings 7:1). Thus, the Lord's response came approximately twelve years after Solomon's prayer and supplication to the Lord during the dedication of the temple.

3. I HAVE CONSECRATED THIS HOUSE: The Lord made the temple holy by being present in the cloud. As proof, the Lord told Solomon that He had put His name there.

MY NAME THERE FOREVER: God was not saying He would dwell in that building forever, as less than 400 years later the Babylonians destroyed it. Rather, He was saying that Jerusalem and the temple mount would be His earthly throne as long as the earth remained. Even after the earth passes away, the Bible tells us there will be the heavenly Jerusalem, where God will eternally dwell (see Revelation 21:1–2).

MY EYES AND MY HEART: These symbolized the Lord's constant attention toward and deep affection for Israel. By implication, He promised them access to His presence and answers to their prayers.

4. IF YOU WALK: The Lord reiterated to Solomon the importance of obedience to the Mosaic statutes in order to experience the blessings of the Davidic covenant.

6. IF YOU OR YOUR SONS AT ALL TURN: God was saying that if Israel ("you" is plural) abandoned the Lord, He would expel them from the land and destroy the temple.

9. THE LORD HAS BROUGHT ALL THIS CALAMITY: Moses had predicted the destruction of Jerusalem and the people's exile from the land (see Deuteronomy 29:24–28). The future devastation of the temple would graphically demonstrate the Lord's anger against Israel's sin—particularly the sin of idolatry.

UNLEASHING THE TEXT

1) How long did it take Solomon to build the temple? What does the attention to detail and the fact "no hammer or chisel or any iron tool was heard at the temple" (1 Kings 6:7) tell you about the sacred nature of the temple construction?

_____

_____

_____

2) What reminder does God give Solomon as he is building the temple (see 6:11–13)? What does this tell you about God's priorities for Israel?

_____

_____

_____

3) How did God show his presence when the ark of covenant was brought into the temple? Why did Solomon remind the people of God's power and faithfulness in the past?

_____

_____

_____

4) How did Solomon describe God in his prayer (see 8:27)? How did he describe the heart Israel needed to have? When God spoke to Solomon after the temple was dedicated, why did He remind Solomon of the importance of being faithful to Him?

_____

_____

_____

EXPLORING THE MEANING

Worship involves sacrifice. Solomon understood the importance of the task he had been given in building the temple, for it represented the place where the people would come to present sacrifices to God. Although the heavens themselves could not contain God (see 1 Kings 8:27), the temple reminded the people that He was always in their midst. Furthermore, the shedding of blood informed the Israelites of the cost of their sins: "According to the law almost all things are purified with blood, and without shedding of blood there is no remission" (Hebrews 9:22).

For Solomon and the people, worshiping God involved making sacrifices in terms of time and resources to build the house for God. It involved making animal sacrifices at the altar so atonement could be made for their sins. It also involved the sacrifice of giving back to God a portion of what He had provided to them—and in this way acknowledging that "every good gift and every perfect gift is from above, and comes down from the Father of lights" (James 1:17).

21

Today, our worship also involves sacrifice. This may involve the sacrifice of our time in reading God's Word, the sacrifice of our finances to help those in need, or the sacrifice of giving up something important to us to show we place God above all else. For some believers, worshiping God may even mean sacrificing their status in society—or their physical safety. God honors all these sacrifices when they are done in true worship: "The sacrifices of God are a broken spirit, a broken and a contrite heart—these, O God, You will not despise" (Psalm 51:17).

Don't confuse activity with obedience. Solomon honored God by building a magnificent temple to His name, but in the end he was less attuned to the purpose of that temple in Israel's midst. Even though God approved of the temple, he reminded Solomon that *faithfulness* to Him was the requirement for his presence—not the temple building itself. "If you or your sons at all turn from following Me . . . I will cut off Israel from the land which I have given them; and this house which I have consecrated for My name I will cast out of My sight" (1 Kings 9:6–7).

As believers in Christ, we can become so wrapped up in doing the things we think will honor God that we fail to live in obedience to His true commands. This was the problem Jesus had with the Pharisees: they were careful to follow the *letter* of the Law but completely missed God's *intent* for giving that Law to them. Jesus said of them, "Woe to you, scribes and Pharisees, hypocrites! For you pay tithe of mint and anise and cummin, and have neglected the weightier matters of the law: justice and mercy and faith" (Matthew 23:23).

The purpose of God's laws and decrees in the Old Testament was to turn the people's hearts toward the Lord and facilitate repentance. When we focus on just the outward acts of religion, our busyness and distraction can actually pull us away from God. However, when our hearts are turned toward God and we are acting according to His will, we will bring Him glory and serve as an example of His love to the world.

God blesses our obedience to His Word. Toward the end of King David's reign, he said to Solomon, "May the LORD be with you; and may you prosper, and build the house of the LORD your God, as He has said to you" (1 Chronicles 22:11). Solomon was faithful to honor this request and build the temple to honor the Lord. As a result, God was faithful to bless Solomon and give him "rest on every side" (1 Kings 5:4). Yet there were conditions for these blessings: "Walk in My statutes, execute My judgments, keep all My commandments" (6:12).

Although God's love is unconditional, the blessings He bestows on us will often be conditional and based on our faithfulness to adhere to His Word. As Proverbs 28:20 states, "A faithful man will abound with blessings, but he who hastens to be rich will not go unpunished." God will allow any lack of faithfulness on our part to lead to consequences, "for whatever a man sows, that he will also reap" (Galatians 6:7).

God will use these consequences to correct us and lead us back to the path of righteousness. The writer of Hebrews summed this up when he said, "No chastening seems to be joyful for the present, but painful; nevertheless, afterward it yields the peaceable fruit of righteousness to those who have been trained by it" (Hebrews 12:11). God's correction is always meant to lead us back to the place of obedience, where He can bless our faithfulness.

REFLECTING ON THE TEXT

5) What are some ways you see honor of God fading in our culture? In Christian churches?

_____

_____

_____

6) What sacrifices might be required to walk faithfully with God? What are the benefits of making those sacrifices?

_____

_____

_____

7) How is being religious different from being a Christian? How can a genuine relationship with God give meaning to "religious" activities?

_____

_____

_____

8) How would you define *blessing*? What is the relationship between faithfulness to God, obedience to His Word, and God's blessings?

_____

_____

_____

PERSONAL RESPONSE

9) How do you honor God? In what ways do you need to honor Him more? How would this impact your knowledge of and relationship with God?

_____

_____

_____

10) In what ways do you need to be more faithful to God? How have you experienced God's blessings for your obedience?

_____

_____

_____

THE DECLINE OF SOLOMON

1 Kings 10:14–11:43

DRAWING NEAR

Think of a time when you had to work with someone who had different morals from you. What issues did you encounter? How did you resolve them?

_____

_____

_____

THE CONTEXT

Solomon began his reign on a high note. He loved the Lord and walked according to His statutes, just as his father had done. The Lord had blessed him not only with great wisdom but also with riches and power. Solomon had continued to walk in obedience to God by taking up the task to build the temple. However, as we have seen, he also continued to offer sacrifices at the "high places," where the Canaanites had worshiped their false gods in the past.

Perhaps Solomon justified the practice because it seemed expedient. After all, it took years to complete the temple in Jerusalem, so it might have seemed more important at the time for the Israelites to continue worshiping the Lord than to worry about the details. But this act of disobedience laid the foundation for future acts of rule-breaking, and those acts of rule-breaking led to his downfall.

The root of Solomon's problem was his marriages. Solomon married a great number of women and had a thousand wives before he was finished. Solomon wed many of these women to establish political alliances that would ensure Israel's peace with neighboring nations. This, too, may have seemed expedient to him at the time, as such unions were common in the world. He might have told himself these mixed marriages with foreigners were just part of being king—a leader dealing with the realities of the world. But these wives captured his heart. Solomon loved them more than he loved God and allowed the high places to continue.

The Lord had forbidden His people to intermarry with the world around them, because He knew these mixed marriages would lead Israel into idolatry. This is exactly what happened to Solomon. Even the wisest man in the world is not exempt from obeying the Word of God.

KEYS TO THE TEXT

Read 1 Kings 10:14–11:43, noting the key words and phrases indicated below.

SOLOMON'S WEALTH: The kingdom of Israel is now at the height of its power and influence in the region, and Solomon reaps the benefits of being in that position.

10:15. THE INCOME OF TRADERS: Solomon received about twenty-five tons of gold each year. Gold also came from tolls and tariffs on traders, revenues from administrators, and taxes from Arabian kings who used caravan routes under Solomon's control.

21. NOT ONE WAS SILVER: The writer used this phrase to show that gold was so plentiful in Solomon's kingdom the value of silver had dropped to nothing.

22. THE KING HAD MERCHANT SHIPS: These "ships of Tarshish" were large, all-weather cargo vessels designed to make long ocean voyages.

25. EACH MAN BROUGHT HIS PRESENT: Many rulers brought presents to Solomon as they sought to buy his wisdom and apply it to their own nations.

These gifts led Solomon to multiply horses for himself, as well as silver and gold, which God had warned kings not to do (see Deuteronomy 17:16–17). Solomon became ensnared by the blessings of his own wisdom and disobeyed God's commands.

28. BOUGHT THEM IN KEVEH: Keveh was in Cilicia, an area south of the Taurus Mountains in Asia Minor. In antiquity, Cilicia was fabled for breeding and selling the best horses.

29. KINGS OF THE HITTITES: The Hittite empire reached the peak of its power in 1380–1350 BC. When it collapsed in 1200 BC, many Hittite city-states developed, each with its own king. These rulers were called "the kings of the Hittites" and were scattered in Solomon's day throughout Anatolia and northern Aram (Syria).

KINGS OF SYRIA: This geographic area was to the north of Judea and had Damascus as its major city. The land was actually known as Aram in Old Testament times.

SOLOMON'S WIVES: King Solomon marries a thousand wives and concubines, many of whom are from foreign nations. This is in violation of the Lord's commands.

11:1. KING SOLOMON LOVED MANY FOREIGN WOMEN: In Solomon's day, having many wives was seen as a sign of wealth and importance. However, by following this practice Solomon violated two of God's laws: taking many wives (see Deuteronomy 17:17), and marrying foreign women (see Deuteronomy 7:1–4). The Lord had warned the Israelites not to marry Canaanites because such unions would lead them into paganism, which was what happened with Solomon.

MOABITES, AMMONITES, EDOMITES, SIDONITES, AND HITTITES: The Moabites and Ammonites lived in the land east of the Dead Sea and were descendants of Lot (see Genesis 19:36–38). The Edomites were located in the region of the Transjordan and were the offspring of Esau (see Genesis 36:1). The Sidonians lived in Sidon, on the shore of the Mediterranean, and the Hittites were spread throughout Syria.

2. YOU SHALL NOT INTERMARRY WITH THEM: The Lord had warned His people not to intermarry with the Gentiles because it would make them "unequally yoked." This same principle applies to Christians today: we are

warned in Scripture not to marry non-believers, because the nonbeliever will lead the believer away from God (see 2 Corinthians 6:14).

SURELY THEY WILL TURN AWAY YOUR HEARTS: Some Christians excuse romantic involvement with non-Christians with the argument they will lead the other person to the Lord. But God here warned the people clearly that it does not work that way. When a Christian is unequally yoked with a non-Christian, the Christian's walk with the Lord generally will suffer.

SOLOMON CLUNG TO THESE IN LOVE: Solomon was the wisest man who ever lived, yet his great wisdom did not prevent him from being led away from the Lord by his pagan wives—even though he may have loved them dearly and would certainly have wanted the best for them. No sadder picture can be imagined than the ugly apostasy of his latter years, which can be traced back to his sins with foreign wives.

4. THE HEART OF HIS FATHER DAVID: David had not led a sinless life, yet the author of 1 Kings consistently presented him as the standard by which other kings were to act and be judged. This was because of the fact that David had repented of his sins, turned his life back to the Lord, and had not allowed sin to continue as a pattern in his life.

SYNCRETISM: Solomon's many wives lead him away from the Lord's prescribed worship, and he begins to add in elements of pagan religions.

5. WENT AFTER ASHTORETH . . . AND AFTER MILCOM: Ashtoreth was the Canaanite goddess of love and fertility. Milcom, also called Molech, was a Canaanite god whose worship practices included child sacrifice "through the fire" (Leviticus 18:21). There is a certain irony that Solomon's wives, whom he loved, led him to worship the pagan goddess of love. The fact he adopted a god whose worship included child sacrifice reveals that he, as the shepherd of God's people, had led Israel away from the Lord.

6. DID NOT FULLY FOLLOW THE LORD: One again, the author notes that Solomon followed the Lord partially but not fully. He obeyed the Lord's Word in some aspects, such as building the temple, but he also indulged in disobedience. The result of this partial obedience was disastrous. The Lord calls His people to complete obedience. He does not give us leeway to pick and choose what parts of His Word we will follow.

7. SOLOMON BUILT A HIGH PLACE FOR CHEMOSH: Chemosh was the god of the Moabites, to whom the sacrifice of children was customary. Solomon had now become an open idolater, worshiping images of wood and stone in sight of the temple that he had previously built to honor God. His partial compliance with God's will had now led to his complete noncompliance.

HILL THAT IS EAST OF JERUSALEM: This is probably the Mount of Olives. This is the area called Tophet in Jeremiah 7:31 and the Mount of Corruption in 2 Kings 23:13.

GOD REJECTS SOLOMON AS KING: *The Lord will not permit the shepherd of His people to adulterate His Word with pagan practices. He becomes angry with Solomon and rejects him as king.*

9. THE LORD BECAME ANGRY WITH SOLOMON: The blessings God had given to Solomon did not exempt him from walking in obedience. Quite the contrary, in fact: the Lord's great generosity made Solomon more accountable to God's commands. The Lord does not pick favorites; all men are called to obey His Word, from the king to the poorest peasant.

APPEARED TO HIM TWICE: God had warned Solomon at Gibeon (see 1 Kings 3:5) and at Jerusalem (see 9:2) to remain faithful to Him, so Solomon had no excuses.

10. HE DID NOT KEEP WHAT THE LORD HAD COMMANDED: Solomon had failed to obey the commandments to honor God (see Exodus 20:3–6), which were part of the Mosaic covenant. Obedience to that covenant was necessary for receiving the blessings of the Davidic covenant.

11. I WILL SURELY TEAR THE KINGDOM AWAY FROM YOU: God had intended the gifts He had given to Solomon to be used for ruling the people, not his own selfish use. Solomon had led God's people astray, so the Lord would take away his throne and remove his descendants from leadership over His people. The Lord's tearing of the kingdom from Solomon would later be announced in Ahijah's symbolic act of tearing his garment (see verses 29–39).

12. FOR THE SAKE OF YOUR FATHER DAVID: The Lord had made an unconditional covenant with David to establish his throne forever (see 2 Samuel 7:12–16). It was through this covenant that God would eventually establish the reign of His Son, Jesus. The Lord had also promised David that He would not remove His mercy from his son, as He had from Saul, effectively promising that

He would not expel Solomon from the throne. Solomon's disobedience did not annul the Davidic covenant, and the Lord's commitment to fulfill His word to David remained firm. Nevertheless, Solomon's dynasty would end when he died.

13. I WILL GIVE ONE TRIBE TO YOUR SON: God was telling Solomon that a great division was coming to Israel, when the nation would split in two, but the tribe of Judah would remain loyal to the house of David. The Lord had chosen Jerusalem as the place where His name would dwell forever; therefore, Jerusalem and the temple would remain so that the divine promise might stand.

SOLOMON'S ADVERSARIES: *God's verdict against Solomon begins to come to fulfillment as two adversaries rise up to challenge Israel's authority in the land.*

14. HADAD THE EDOMITE: The Lord had given David many great victories over Israel's enemies, including the Edomites (see 2 Samuel 8:13–14). Hadad belonged to the royal family that had ruled Edom, and he escaped death as a child by being taken to Egypt.

18. FROM MIDIAN . . . TO PARAN: Midian was the land directly east of Edom, where Hadad first fled on his way to Egypt. Paran was a wilderness southeast of Kadesh in the central area of the Sinai Peninsula.

21. LET ME DEPART: When Hadad heard of the deaths of David and Joab, he renounced his position and possessions in Egypt to return to Edom so as to regain his throne. His activities gave great trouble to Israel.

23. REZON THE SON OF ELIADAH: After David conquered Zobar (see 2 Samuel 8:3–8), Rezon and his men took Damascus and established the strong dynasty of Syrian kings that would trouble the Israelites during the ninth century BC.

REBELLION: *Solomon soon not only has to deal with external threats to his kingdom but also internal threats when Jeroboam, a trusted servant, rebels against him.*

26. JEROBOAM THE SON OF NEBAT: In contrast to Hadad and Rezon, who were external adversaries of Solomon, God raised up Jeroboam from a town in Ephraim as an internal adversary. Jeroboam was from Ephraim, the

leading tribe of Israel's ten northern tribes. He was a young man of talent and energy who, having been appointed by Solomon as leader over the building works around Jerusalem, rose to public notice.

28. THE LABOR FORCE: This labor force was comprised of 30,000 Israelites who worked in Lebanon. For every month they worked, they were off two months, which meant they worked only four months per year. They performed the task of felling trees.

29. AHIJAH THE SHILONITE: Ahijah was a prophet of the Lord who lived in Shiloh, a town in Ephraim about twenty miles north of Jerusalem.

31. HE SAID TO JEROBOAM: In this monumental prophecy, God proclaimed that because of Solomon's sins, the kingdom would be divided and Jeroboam would rule in the northern area.

36. A LAMP BEFORE ME: A lighted lamp represented the life of an individual (see Job 18:6; Psalm 132:17). God again promised that David, from the tribe of Judah, would continue to have descendants who ruled in Jerusalem.

38. IF YOU HEED ALL THAT I COMMAND YOU: God gave the same promise to Jeroboam that He had given to David—he would have an enduring royal dynasty over Israel, the ten northern tribes, if he obeyed God's Law. The Lord also imposed the same conditions on Jeroboam for his kingship that He had imposed on David.

39. BUT NOT FOREVER: This statement implied the kingdom's division was not to be permanent and that David's house would ultimately rule all the tribes of Israel again.

40. SOLOMON THEREFORE SOUGHT TO KILL JEROBOAM: Although the prophecy was private, Solomon heard about it and set out to kill Jeroboam. The end of Solomon's reign thus bore a striking similarity to that of Saul's reign. God had rejected both kings, and when the Lord selected the man who would be the next king, Saul and Solomon both responded by trying to murder that chosen one. The fact that Solomon would try to kill the Lord's anointed successor demonstrated just how far his heart had strayed from God.

SHISHAK KING OF EGYPT: Shishak was the founder of the twenty-second dynasty in Egypt and reigned c. 945–924 BC. He would later invade Judah during the reign of Rehoboam.

42. SOLOMON REIGNED IN JERUSALEM . . . FORTY YEARS: Solomon reigned from 971–931 BC.

UNLEASHING THE TEXT

1) What might have been Solomon's reasons for marrying so many women? How might he have justified it in his own mind?

_____

_____

_____

2) What role did Solomon's marriages play in his downfall? How might his life have ended differently if he had not married foreigners?

_____

_____

_____

3) Why did God become angry with Solomon? What specifically had Solomon done wrong?

_____

_____

_____

4) Why is it dangerous for a Christian to marry a non-Christian? What causes the Christian to be led astray by the non-Christian, rather than vice versa?

_____

_____

_____

EXPLORING THE MEANING

Christians should not marry non-Christians. God warned His people repeatedly in the Old Testament not to marry those who did not obey His Word. He had specifically advised the Israelites as they were leaving Egypt not to give their sons and daughters to the people of Canaan (see Deuteronomy 7:1–3). The primary reason for these injunctions was that such marriages would cause God's people to drift away from obedience and into idolatry.

Christians today sometimes argue that they can lead a non-Christian spouse to salvation, and they use that logic to justify an unequal union. Such thinking is misguided, however, for God's Word warns consistently that the opposite will prove true: the unbeliever will lead the believer away from God. "Take heed to yourself, lest you make a covenant with the inhabitants of the land where you are going, lest it be a snare in your midst" (Exodus 34:12).

In Paul's second letter to the Corinthians, he uses the metaphor of two oxen sharing a yoke to explain what a union between Christians is like. If a Christian marries a non-Christian, it is like yoking two animals together that want to pull in opposite directions—and such an arrangement can only lead to disaster. Paul cautioned, "Do not be unequally yoked together with unbelievers. For what fellowship has righteousness with lawlessness? And what communion has light with darkness? . . . Or what part has a believer with an unbeliever?" (6:14–15). God's people must not intermarry with those who are not part of His body.

God calls His people to complete obedience. As we have seen, Solomon began well. He loved God and followed His laws, just as his father had done. But, as we have also seen, there was one problem. "Solomon loved the LORD, walking in the statutes of his father David, *except* that he sacrificed and burned incense at the high places" (1 Kings 3:3, emphasis added). Solomon had laid a trap for himself early in his life, and now we see the terrible fruit of the decision.

Solomon had compromised by thinking there was an area of his life that was somehow exempt from obedience to the Lord's statutes. God's people were not to offer sacrifices on the high places—their worship was to be conducted at the temple in Jerusalem. But Solomon did not follow that principle and continued to offer sacrifices at sites that had been used to worship pagan gods. As he grew older, his disobedience turned his heart away from serving God: "His heart was not loyal to the LORD his God, as was the heart of his father David" (1 Kings 11:4).

33

Walking with the Lord requires obedience on our part, and we are not given freedom to handpick which areas of His Word we will obey and which we will ignore. It is *all* for our good. "For the word of God is living and powerful, and sharper than any two-edged sword, piercing even to the division of soul and spirit, and of joints and marrow, and is a discerner of the thoughts and intents of the heart" (Hebrews 4:12). "All Scripture is given by inspiration of God, and is profitable for doctrine, for reproof, for correction, for instruction in righteousness, that the man of God may be complete, thoroughly equipped for every good work" (2 Timothy 3:16–17).

The Lord does not tolerate syncretism. Syncretism is the act of combining elements of diverse religious philosophies into a new form of worship. Solomon attempted to do this when he added pagan practice to the prescribed worship of God, drawing in elements from the worship of a variety of false gods. The Lord had expressly forbidden His people from intermarrying for this very reason, and Solomon's paganism led to the loss of his kingdom.

The modern church has frequently fallen into syncretism as well, incorporating worldly principles and ideas into the Word of God. This can be seen in the addition of New Age ideas, evolutionary thinking, self-help approaches to sinful behaviors, or pandering to cultural trends. Christians act in an unwise manner when they attempt to add to the written Word of God, because it is complete already and as pertinent today as when it was first written.

As we will see during the course of these studies, the world offers a form of wisdom that can appear sound at first glance, but its source is not from God. This "wisdom" is from below, not from above. Christians must be constantly on guard to prevent such false wisdom from being added to the sound teachings of Scripture.

REFLECTING ON THE TEXT

5) What worldly teachings or philosophies have found their way into church practices today?

_____

_____

_____

6) Solomon evidently genuinely loved his wives. Why was that tenderness not enough to prevent him from going astray? How does this principle apply in modern times?

_____

_____

_____

7) How does God's injunction against unequal yoking apply to other relationships besides marriage—such as friendships, church membership, or business dealings?

_____

_____

_____

8) How does a Christian reach out to the unsaved while avoiding unequal yoking? How is this balance achieved?

_____

_____

_____

PERSONAL RESPONSE

9) Are there areas in your life in which you are not walking in complete obedience? What will you do this week to change that?

_____

_____

_____

10) Are there people in your life who are leading you away from a close walk with God? What will you do about those relationships?

_____

_____

_____

4

THE WISDOM OF THE PROVERBS

Proverbs 1:1–6; 2:1–22; 4:1–27

DRAWING NEAR

What are some of the "proverbs" your parents taught you when you were growing up?

_____

_____

_____

THE CONTEXT

As we saw in our first study, God had given Solomon such great wisdom that he was deemed to be the wisest man of all time. People from all across the land traveled great distances to learn from him and give him gifts to try to secure his wisdom. During his lifetime, he spoke 3,000 proverbs and wrote more than 1,000 songs (see 1 Kings 4:30–34). For the rest of this study, we will focus on his writings in the books of Proverbs and Ecclesiastes.

A *proverb* is a short, pithy saying that expresses a general principle of life and often gives advice on how to live wisely. Modern American examples include, "an apple a day keeps the doctor away," "a penny saved is a penny earned," and "all that glitters is not gold." The book of Proverbs is a collection of such wise sayings that teach us, in practical terms, how to gain understanding and live with wisdom. Note that these were not necessarily intended as *prophecies* or *promises*, but general principles by which people should live.

Solomon wrote the vast majority of the proverbs himself, but the Bible indicates there were other authors as well. For instance, certain sections in Proverbs refer to "sayings of the wise" (see 22:17–21; 24:23), which indicates the writings came from a circle of wise men. Proverbs 30 is attributed to "Agur the son of Jakeh," and Proverbs 31:1–9 is attributed to "King Lemuel." This king might have been Solomon himself, though certain Aramaic spellings in his sayings may point to an individual with a non-Israelite background.

Most of the proverbs consist of succinct observations about life. Many teach wisdom by contrasting opposites, such as the wise man versus the fool or the diligent person versus the sluggard. Solomon began the book, however, with insights into the value of wisdom itself. He warned his reader there was some work involved in attaining true wisdom, but the rewards to be gained were more precious than gold.

KEYS TO THE TEXT

Read Proverbs 1:1–6, noting the key words and phrases indicated below.

THE PURPOSE OF THE PROVERBS: Solomon opens the book of Proverbs with an overview of what the reader is to take away from the wisdom contained in this writing.

1:1. THE PROVERBS OF SOLOMON: Proverbs contain insights both in poetry and prose, yet at the same time they can be commands to be obeyed. Proverbs in the Bible are not limited to this book alone (see 1 Samuel 10:12; 24:13; Ezekiel 12:22; 18:2).

2. TO KNOW WISDOM: The twofold purpose of Proverbs is (1) to produce the skill of godly living in the reader by wisdom and instruction, and (2) to help that individual develop discernment. To the Hebrew mind, *wisdom* was not knowledge alone but the skill of living as God intended humans to live. *Instruction* refers to the discipline of the moral nature, while *understanding* involves the mental discipline that matures a person for spiritual discernment.

THE WISDOM OF THE PROVERBS

3. JUSTICE, JUDGMENT, AND EQUITY: *Justice* is the ability to conform to the will and standard of God—a practical righteousness that matches one's positional righteousness. *Judgment* is the application of true righteousness in dealing with others. *Equity* is the practice of leading one's life in a fair and pleasing way.

4. PRUDENCE TO THE SIMPLE: An additional purpose of Proverbs is to impart discernment to the naïve and the ignorant. The root of *simple* is a word meaning an open door, which is an apt description of those who do not know what to keep in or out of their minds. The goal is for the reader to ponder the words so as to make a decision that does not lead to sin.

6. A PROVERB AND AN ENIGMA: These proverbs seek to sharpen the reader's mind by schooling in "parabolic speech" and "dark sayings" that need reflection and interpretation. The study of the Scriptures is sufficient to provide wisdom for the perplexities of life.

Read Proverbs 2:1–22, noting the key words and phrases indicated below.

SEEK, SEARCH, CRY OUT: *The process of gaining wisdom requires deliberate effort on our part.*

2:1. RECEIVE MY WORDS, AND TREASURE MY COMMANDS: Solomon had embraced God's law and made it his own by faith and obedience as well as teaching. Three steps were necessary for those who wished to receive his words and become wise. First, the person must be willing to receive or hear instruction from another who is wiser. Second, the person must value wisdom as more precious than treasure. Third, as we will see in this and future studies, the person must act on those wise teachings. It is not enough for a person to merely listen and learn; he or she must also obey if he or she is to become wise.

2. YOUR EAR TO WISDOM . . . YOUR HEART TO UNDERSTANDING: Once wisdom is properly valued, both the ear and mind are captivated by it. *Wisdom* in this sense means "skill" and refers to the quality that enables a person to live life skillfully, avoiding the world's countless traps and pitfalls. *Understanding* refers to one's mind, specifically the intellectual discipline required to gain wisdom. God calls His people to work toward a deep understanding of His Word and to apply that Word in their lives. These things lead to wisdom.

3. CRY OUT: This suggests one must desire wisdom—to the point of crying out—in order to obtain it, for the least bit of indifference will leave one bereft of the fullness of wisdom. Yet this verse also reminds us that true wisdom comes only from God, and all we need to do is ask Him to give it to us. "If any of you lacks wisdom, let him ask of God, who gives to all liberally and without reproach, and it will be given to him" (James 1:5).

4. SEEK HER . . . AND SEARCH: We are to ask the Lord for wisdom, but we are also to *seek* or *search* for it. Part of the seeking step is an act of faith: "Let him ask in faith, with no doubting, for he who doubts is like a wave of the sea driven and tossed by the wind" (James 1:6). The seeking or searching also encompasses obedience, for obtaining wisdom requires us to obey what we understand from God's Word.

SOME BENEFITS OF WISDOM: Wisdom and understanding bring benefits to those who possess them.

5. THE KNOWLEDGE OF GOD: Knowledge of God comes through having a close and personal relationship with Him, which is available to everyone through Jesus. Those who are redeemed by the blood of Christ are "upright" and continue to walk in obedience to His Word.

6. FROM HIS MOUTH: The words from God's mouth are contained in Scripture. "God, who at various times and in various ways spoke in time past to the fathers by the prophets, has in these last days spoken to us by His Son" (Hebrews 1:1–2). It is there that God speaks.

7. SOUND WISDOM FOR THE UPRIGHT: This identifies those who are true believers—those who seek to know, love, and obey God and live righteously. These covenant keepers alone can know wisdom and experience God's protection.

9. RIGHTEOUSNESS AND JUSTICE, EQUITY: True *righteousness* can only come through the sacrificial death and resurrection of Jesus Christ. It is a gift freely bestowed on all who believe in Christ and cannot be earned by anyone's good works. On a different level, however, righteousness can refer to acts of obedience to God's Word, as it does here. *Justice* is a quality of God's character, and those who behave justly are acting in a godly manner. *Equity* refers to fairness and impartiality—the quality of treating all people on an equal level. This is also a trait of God's character, who is no respecter of persons (see Romans 2:11).

10. WHEN WISDOM ENTERS YOUR HEART: Wisdom is not mere head knowledge; it is a practical daily lifestyle—a living out of the principles of God's Word. It must enter one's heart in the sense that practical obedience must become a constant habit if one is to become wise.

11. DISCRETION: This is the quality of being able to discern what course of action is right and fitting. It is similar to prudence, which is another quality found in the book of Proverbs.

HOW WISDOM PROTECTS: *Wisdom not only brings benefits to the person who follows her guidance but also protects that person from the evil enticements of the world.*

12. DELIVER YOU FROM THE WAY OF EVIL: The world is full of those who preach false doctrine, urging us to depart from obedience to God's Word. Wisdom enables us to recognize such false teachings and avoid those who speak perversely.

16. DELIVER YOU FROM THE IMMORAL WOMAN: Literally "foreign" or "strange" woman, because such individuals at first were from outside Israel. Eventually, this came to include any prostitute or adulteress. The book of Proverbs refers to this immoral woman repeatedly, but the principles can be applied just as easily to a wayward man, as any form of sexual immorality leads only to destruction.

17. FORGETS THE COVENANT OF HER GOD: In a wider sense this could be the covenant of Sinai (see Exodus 20:14), but here it refers to a marriage covenant—a sacred vow made in the presence of God. "Therefore a man shall leave his father and mother and be joined to his wife, and they shall become one flesh" (Genesis 2:24). The Bible forbids any sexual behavior apart from the marriage covenant.

18. HER HOUSE LEADS DOWN TO DEATH: The destructive nature of sexual sin leads a person to walk alongside death. Death in the book of Proverbs is presented as both a gradual descent (see 5:23) and a sudden end (see 29:1).

19. NONE WHO GO TO HER RETURN: The irreversible nature of continuing in sexual sin points to its devastating consequences. It leads to physical death, for "the wicked will be cut off from the earth, and the unfaithful will be uprooted from it" (verse 22). After that comes the reality of eternal death.

21. THE UPRIGHT WILL DWELL IN THE LAND: However, unlike those who live in sexual sin and are headed for death, those who belong to the Lord will live.

Read Proverbs 4:1–27, noting the key words and phrases indicated below.

IN ALL YOUR GETTING: Life is filled with obligations and demands, but Christians must always keep wisdom as their top priority.

4:2. GOOD DOCTRINE: The Word of God is the source of all true wisdom. Any counsel that goes against God's Word is not genuine wisdom.

3. I WAS MY FATHER'S SON: God commanded His people to train their children in His laws. In Deuteronomy 6:7, He said to the people, "You shall teach [My law] diligently to your children, and shall talk of them when you sit in your house, when you walk by the way, when you lie down, and when you rise up." This principle still applies today: parents should be diligent to train their children in godly wisdom.

5. DO NOT FORGET: Wisdom is not something one acquires once and for all; being wise requires daily refreshing from the Word of God. It is too easy to forget true wisdom when we allow our lives to become cluttered with the things of this world. Those who wish to become wise must constantly be immersing themselves in Scripture and godly teaching.

7. IN ALL YOUR GETTING: Life is filled with "getting"—getting a paycheck, getting an education, getting groceries, and on and on. However, it is easy to become obsessed with getting as we accumulate possessions and strive to advance in career or social circles. Solomon warned us to make our first priority getting wisdom and understanding.

8. WHEN YOU EMBRACE HER: This metaphor implies deep intimacy and suggests the marital embrace between a man and wife. The wise man has a deep love for God's ways, and he takes His Word into the most intimate parts of his life.

12. YOUR STEPS WILL NOT BE HINDERED: People in Solomon's day wore long, flowing garments that could become entangled on their feet while walking or running. To guard against this, people would hitch up their robes and secure them under their belts. The image here suggests that life's concerns and temptations can also trip us up, but wisdom will help us make safe paths for our feet.

13. TAKE FIRM HOLD OF INSTRUCTION: Notice the imperatives in this verse: "take firm hold," "do not let go," "keep her." If we consider true wisdom as being more valuable than gold or gems, we will be determined to hang on to it at all costs.

THE ENEMY OF OUR SOULS: We must not lose sight of the fact that the devil and the world system are constantly warring against God's people.

14. THE PATH OF THE WICKED: The book of Proverbs frequently presents the reader with two choices: the way of evil and the way of wisdom. The world teaches that life is complicated, that most decisions are shades of gray, and that there are many paths from which to choose. However, God's Word teaches there are only two ways to choose from: the wicked ways of the world and the wise ways of God. Anything that does not adhere to the teachings of Scripture is part of the path of the wicked.

15. AVOID . . . TRAVEL . . . TURN . . . PASS: Four verbs identify the necessary steps in urgently dealing with sin at its inception: (1) avoid the sinful situation, (2) travel as far from it as possible, (3) turn away from the sin, and (4) pass beyond or escape the sin.

16. THEY DO NOT SLEEP: The wicked have to sin before they can sleep, and they view their sin as food for their hungry souls. Life is not merely a passive series of choices; we have an enemy who actively seeks our destruction. The devil uses tactics and devices to lead us away from God, and he is always at work against us. Those who do not actively follow the paths of righteousness inevitably follow the path of wickedness, and they end up doing the devil's work.

18. PATH OF THE JUST IS LIKE THE SHINING SUN: The path of the believer is one of increasing light, just as a sunrise begins with the faint glow of dawn and proceeds to the splendor of noonday. The way of the wicked is like darkness, for sin can be so blinding that the wicked trip over the obvious. They are like ones who walk in pitch darkness without any light whatsoever.

19. THEY DO NOT KNOW WHAT MAKES THEM STUMBLE: This can be seen in the world around us, as people pursue ungodliness and then are puzzled at the inevitable results.

23. KEEP YOUR HEART: That is, we must guard our minds, for whatever we take into our minds will influence our speech and behavior. For this reason, it is vital for Christians to steep their minds in Scripture.

UNLEASHING THE TEXT

1) What are some of the rewards and benefits of wisdom?

_____

_____

_____

2) Define each of the following terms and give some practical examples.

Wisdom:

_____

_____

_____

_____

Instruction:

_____

_____

_____

Understanding:

_____

_____

_____

_____

Justice:

_____

_____

_____

Equity:

_____

_____

_____

3) Why does Solomon warn us not to forget wisdom? What causes this to happen? How can it be avoided?

_____

_____

_____

_____

4) What does it mean to "embrace" wisdom? How is this done? Why is it important?

_____

_____

_____

EXPLORING THE MEANING

Gaining wisdom requires effort. Great athletes understand it takes hard work to excel in their sport. Wealthy people will acknowledge readily that money does not grow on trees but requires diligence and shrewdness to attain. Practically any field of endeavor necessitates hard work if a person is to advance—and wisdom is no exception.

This is balanced, of course, with the fact that God gives wisdom as a free gift to those who ask. He is the source of all true wisdom, and no one can become wise apart from Him. Yet wisdom and understanding also require diligent effort on our part: the effort of obedience to God's Word and diligence in studying His Word. We must put God's Word into practice if we want to gain wisdom.

Nevertheless, it is well worth the effort, for wisdom pays large dividends. There are the temporary rewards of honor and longevity mentioned in Proverbs, but the real benefit of wisdom is eternal: the more one lives in wisdom, the more he becomes like Christ. Nothing else on earth is of more value than that.

Life presents a choice: wisdom or folly. Life in this fallen world offers countless options that lead away from God and toward destruction, but in reality there are only two paths: the path of wisdom or the path of folly. While the world has all manner of counsel and advice, everything it offers is, in fact, on the same path. It all leads to destruction.

So-called "wisdom" that is from the world is easier to obtain and easier to follow than wisdom that comes from God. For this reason, the path of the world is wide, and it seems as if everyone is on it. But the path of true wisdom is narrow, and there are few who find it. Consider how Jesus described it: "Wide is the gate and broad is the way that leads to destruction, and there are many who go in by it" (Matthew 7:13). This is contrasted with the path of wisdom: "Narrow is the gate and difficult is the way which leads to life, and there are few who find it" (verse 14).

Fortunately, we are not alone! God gives His Spirit to Christians to indwell us, teach us the wisdom from above, and enable us to live with skill and become more like Christ. He is the Counselor, the one who shows us all things that are true and who enables us to follow the path of wisdom.

Parents should deliberately teach their children in the ways of wisdom. Wisdom does not come naturally to children. Quite the contrary, in fact. Proverbs tells us that "foolishness is bound up in the heart of a child" (22:15), which reminds us that all humans are born sinners and foolish behavior comes naturally to us all. This same verse, however, teaches us to replace a child's folly with wisdom by using "the rod of correction."

This "rod of correction" includes far more than corporal punishment. David imparted wisdom to Solomon by teaching him from God's law. He also modeled wisdom for his son, demonstrating by his own lifestyle what it meant to be a man after God's own heart. This did not mean David was perfect—the Bible records grievous sins in his life, including, as mentioned previously, his early relations with Bathsheba, Solomon's mother.

No Christian parent is perfect. We all wrestle with our sin, and so we all make bad decisions from time to time. Yet David's success in teaching wisdom to Solomon demonstrates that God uses sinners to teach other sinners His ways. This is especially true of parents and their children, for God's Word makes it clear that parents have a responsibility to train up their children in the ways of wisdom.

REFLECTING ON THE TEXT

5) Why did Solomon place such stress on searching and crying out for wisdom? What part do our efforts play in gaining wisdom? What part does God play?

_____

_____

_____

6) What is the "path of the wicked" (Proverbs 4:14)? What is the "path of righteousness" (Proverbs 2:20)? How does one discern between the two paths?

_____

_____

_____

7) What does it mean to "keep your heart with all diligence" (Proverbs 4:23)? How is this done? Why is it important?

_____

_____

_____

8) What tactics does the world use to lead people away from wisdom? What tactics does Satan use? Give practical examples.

_____

_____

_____

PERSONAL RESPONSE

9) How well are you teaching wisdom to others in your life, such as your children? Which speaks louder: your words or your actions?

_____

_____

_____

10) How much do you value wisdom in your own life? What things compete most insistently for your attentions and efforts?

_____

_____

_____

5

SPEAKING WITH WISDOM

Proverbs 5:1–8; 10:10–32; 15:1–7, 23–33

DRAWING NEAR

When is a time that speaking without thinking got you into trouble? What did you need to do to resolve the situation?

_____

_____

_____

THE CONTEXT

"Talk is cheap," the saying goes, implying that words are not as important as actions. In some instances this can be true, yet it belies an important fact that Scripture emphasizes: our words do matter. Jesus confirmed this when He commanded His disciples, "Let your 'Yes' be 'Yes,' and your 'No,' 'No'" (Matthew 5:37). And James warned his readers, "The tongue is a fire, a world of iniquity" (James 3:6). Our words have tremendous power—both for good and for evil.

We worship a God who created the universe by the power of His word. When God speaks, everything in the universe obeys, and Jesus Himself is described as being "the Word" (John 1:1). In fact, one of the ways people are distinguished from the lower orders of creation is by the power of speech. We were given language as a gift from God, and He expects us to use that gift to glorify the One who gave it.

The book of Proverbs is filled with admonitions on how to use speech correctly, along with warnings concerning those who use their words for evil. Proverbs tells us that the wise person will be one whose words are filled with knowledge and understanding. The fool, by contrast, will be one who has no understanding, because he has cut himself off from the source of all knowledge: the God who created him.

In this study, we will learn what it means to use our gift of language wisely, and we will also discover that wise speech can help a person grow in wisdom.

KEYS TO THE TEXT

Read Proverbs 5:1–8, noting the key words and phrases indicated below.

> LIPS OF KNOWLEDGE—OR HONEY: *Solomon opens his teachings by reminding us that our speech influences our behavior—and he contrasts it with the speech of an adulteress.*

5:1. MY SON . . . LEND YOUR EAR: This chapter, like most of Proverbs, is written as instruction from a father to his youthful son. The principles of wisdom it contains, however, apply equally to men and women of any age. The father's command to "lend your ear" reveals that we gain wisdom only by being willing to learn and apply ourselves to hearing wise instruction.

2. PRESERVE DISCRETION . . . KEEP KNOWLEDGE: *Discretion* comes from a Latin word meaning "separation." It implies the ability to separate right from wrong and distinguish wisdom from folly. The person who has discretion is able to discern the wise course of action in any given situation. The wise person will also "keep knowledge," which reminds us that wise speech is a skill that can be lost if we are not diligent to pursue it.

3. THE LIPS OF AN IMMORAL WOMAN DRIP HONEY: In contrast to the wise person, the immoral woman's speech is dripping with honey. Honey is sweet—cloyingly sweet—but it lacks substance, while wise speech is substantially

endowed with knowledge. Elsewhere, though, Solomon pointed out that such sweet speech has a place—within the proper bounds of marriage. "Your lips, O my spouse, drip as the honeycomb; honey and milk are under your tongue" (Song of Solomon 4:11).

HER MOUTH IS SMOOTHER THAN OIL: In other words, her words are slick with flattery and lies.

4. BITTER AS WORMWOOD, SHARP AS A TWO-EDGED SWORD: Wormwood is a bitter plant that grows in desolate areas. It symbolizes the bitterness and desolation that inevitably result from sexual promiscuity. The adulteress's seduction begins sweet and smooth, but it ends in bitterness, violence, and death.

FEET THAT RUSH TO DESTRUCTION: The adulteress's feet lead her away from her home and out into the streets. The feet of the fool lead him to the grave.

5. HER FEET GO DOWN TO DEATH: The book of Proverbs speaks frequently about one's feet, which represent the direction in which one is walking. The fool sets his feet in motion when he listens to the words of the adulteress and follows them to death and destruction.

6. HER WAYS ARE UNSTABLE: That is, the adulteress is shifty and inconsistent, making her ways incomprehensible to the one whom she seduces. The sense is also that she is unstable to avoid thinking about her inevitable destination. She deliberately avoids considering her ways because she does not want to face the pit that lies before her.

7. DO NOT DEPART FROM THE WORDS OF MY MOUTH: Again we are reminded that the wise must continually choose to listen to the godly words of instruction. As we have seen, Solomon's own life demonstrated that a wise man *can* depart from wisdom.

8. REMOVE YOUR WAY FAR FROM HER: Some temptations are unavoidable, but there are things we can do to protect ourselves. The person who wants to avoid the lies of the adulteress can begin by avoiding the situations that lead to hearing those words. We see this in the life of Joseph who, when tempted to commit adultery with Potiphar's wife, "left his garment in her hand, and fled and ran outside" (Genesis 39:12).

Read Proverbs 10:10–32, noting the key words and phrases indicated below.

> SPEAKING IN LOVE: *The wise person will speak the truth at all times, but his words will be tempered with love.*

10:10. HE WHO WINKS WITH THE EYE: That is, one who hints and makes insinuations while not openly making any accusations that can be verified or refuted. Such communication can destroy another person's reputation without any risk to the accuser.

A PRATING FOOL: One who chatters incessantly.

11. A WELL OF LIFE: The wise person's speech leads others toward righteousness and eternal life by encouraging them to godliness and reminding them of the gospel.

12. LOVE COVERS ALL SINS: The hateful person spreads abroad ill reports of his enemies, which "stirs up strife." The wise person does not repeat such gossip, thus covering another person's transgressions with love. Peter would later quote this verse when he wrote, "Above all things have fervent love for one another, for 'love will cover a multitude of sins'" (1 Peter 4:8).

13. FOUND ON THE LIPS OF HIM WHO HAS UNDERSTANDING: Notice there is a connection between understanding and wisdom. The person who speaks with wisdom is circumspect and first considers a matter before commenting on it. Understanding comes from a diligent study of God's Word, while wisdom comes from consistent obedience to the Word. The two operate together to give one wise speech.

DEVOID OF UNDERSTANDING: Fools, by contrast, do not consider their ways or examine their lives in light of God's Word. Their speech is therefore mere empty prattle. They might consider themselves to be wise, but the rod of correction awaits them.

14. WISE PEOPLE STORE UP KNOWLEDGE: This storehouse is filled up from the study of Scripture. As our storehouse of knowledge grows, it will overflow into wise words.

THE MOUTH OF THE FOOLISH IS NEAR DESTRUCTION: The wise person is reticent and determined to think carefully before answering. The fool, however, is quick to respond, even though he is devoid of wisdom. His words will bring about his own destruction.

18. WHOEVER HIDES HATRED . . . WHOEVER SPREADS SLANDER:
It is wrong to both harbor hatred and vent it. Slander (gossip or lies) is also
forbidden.

19. HE WHO RESTRAINS HIS LIPS IS WISE: A wise person restrains his
tongue because he knows speaking too much may cause him to fall into sin. "I
will guard my ways, lest I sin with my tongue; I will restrain my mouth with a
muzzle, while the wicked are before me" (Psalm 39:1).

20. THE TONGUE OF THE RIGHTEOUS . . . THE HEART OF THE WICKED:
Solomon uses these words as parallel terms because they are inseparably
linked. Jesus would later say, "Those things which proceed out of the mouth
come from the heart, and they defile a man" (Matthew 15:18). Good words,
however, are like "choice silver" because they are scarce, precious, and valuable.

21. THE LIPS OF THE RIGHTEOUS FEED . . . BUT FOOLS DIE FOR LACK
OF WISDOM: Sound teaching "feeds" and provides benefits to all, but the fool
starves himself to death spiritually by his lack of wise teaching. "My people are
destroyed for lack of knowledge" (Hosea 4:6).

32. THE LIPS OF THE RIGHTEOUS KNOW WHAT IS ACCEPTABLE: Those
who walk in righteousness are able to determine what is acceptable to God and
speak His truth to others (see Colossians 4:6).

Read Proverbs 15:1–7 and 23–33, noting the key words and phrases indicated
below.

> SPEAKING WITH KNOWLEDGE: *The wise person's speech will also
> be filled with knowledge drawn from the storehouse of Scripture.*

15:1. A SOFT ANSWER TURNS AWAY WRATH: We can use words both to
build up and tear down. A gentle answer, which comes from a heart of love, can
stop a war before it even begins. It can defuse any anger that exists, but harsh
words can actually create anger where none existed before.

2. USES KNOWLEDGE RIGHTLY: It is important to notice there is a right
way and a wrong way to use knowledge. God gives us knowledge, understanding, and wisdom so we may become more like Christ and help others become
more like Him as well. The right way to use knowledge, therefore, is to apply
it to ourselves first and then gently help others move toward godliness. It is

wrong to use knowledge for self-aggrandizement or for browbeating others. The temptation to use knowledge wrongly is perhaps why Paul said that "knowledge puffs up, but love edifies" (1 Corinthians 8:1).

3. EYES OF THE LORD: This refers to God's omniscience. "The LORD looks from heaven; He sees all the sons of men. From the place of His dwelling He looks on all the inhabitants of the earth; He fashions their hearts individually; He considers all their works" (Psalm 33:13–15).

4. A WHOLESOME TONGUE IS A TREE OF LIFE: A wholesome tongue is a "tree of life" in that it speaks words that nurture and bring healing. The Lord God planted the Tree of Life in the Garden of Eden to bring eternal life to the eater (see Genesis 2), and He will use our wise words to lead people toward eternal life. However, when we speak as fools, we bring perverseness into our conversation, just as the serpent did when he lied to Eve and led her astray. Our words can either lead people toward Christ or away from Him—there is no neutral ground.

7. DISPERSE KNOWLEDGE: The wise person's speech will be seasoned with his knowledge of God's character and His Word. He will use knowledge rightly (see verse 2).

SPEAKING AT THE RIGHT TIME: Wise people will act justly and share their wisdom at the right time to build up another person and set him or her on the right course.

23. A WORD SPOKEN IN DUE SEASON, HOW GOOD IT IS: This refers to words of wisdom given at the right moment and when the other person most needs it for edification.

27. HE WHO HATES BRIBES WILL LIVE: In Deuteronomy 16:19, God told His people, "You shall not . . . take a bribe, for a bribe blinds the eyes of the wise and twists the words of the righteous." God forbade His people from accepting bribes because it perverted the ability of judges to act in fairness to both parties.

28. THE MOUTH OF THE WICKED POURS FORTH EVIL: Wicked people don't guard their words, while the wise are a model of restraint and humility, speaking what they know to be true at the appropriate time.

30. LIGHT OF THE EYES . . . A GOOD REPORT: Whatever is good—whatever is sound truth and wisdom—stirs the heart by relieving anxiety and producing a cheerful face.

31. THE EAR THAT HEARS: Once again, acquiring wisdom requires a teachable spirit.

Going Deeper

Read James 3:1–12, noting the key words and phrases indicated below.

SPEAKING LIKE WILDFIRE: James warns us that our tongues are an unruly evil, set on fire by the flames of hell. The wise person will strive for mastery of the tongue.

3:1. LET NOT MANY OF YOU BECOME TEACHERS: The word *teachers* refers to those who preach and teach in an official capacity, such as pastors of local churches. Nevertheless, the principle applies to any Christian who teaches others about godliness, including parents who instruct their children. When we teach, we are expected to live according to the same doctrines we instruct others to follow. God is the one who holds people accountable to this higher standard. Wise speech brings with it a responsibility to live in obedience to God's Word.

2. WE ALL STUMBLE: That is, we all make mistakes continually. This refers to sinful behavior—anything that offends the holiness of God—and speech may be the easiest area in which to fall short of God's glory. It is human nature for us to speak glibly without much thought; yet that is precisely the time when we are most likely to say inappropriate things.

A PERFECT MAN: In biblical times, the word *perfect* often meant "mature." The mature believer will have control over the tongue, using words to encourage others toward godliness. Conversely, this also suggests how hard it is to keep one's tongue under strict control. No one is perfect, and everyone says things, at least now and then, that are not godly.

BRIDLE THE WHOLE BODY: People who gain mastery over their own tongue will also be strong enough in godliness to control their whole body. James was suggesting that the tongue is the weakest member of our bodies, yet the most unruly. Therefore, it should be a primary focus of our efforts toward godliness.

3. BITS IN HORSES' MOUTHS: The horse is a powerful beast, yet it is brought completely under the rider's domination by controlling its tongue. This image suggests that whatever force controls one's tongue will control the whole person—whether that is the sinful nature or the Holy Spirit.

4. DRIVEN BY FIERCE WINDS: James used both ships and horses to demonstrate how the entire body is guided by the tongue. Our tongue can be driven by fierce passions, just as a ship is driven by winds, which can lead to actions. Yet this also suggests our tongue can be controlled by the Holy Spirit, who will guide it toward godliness at all times. When the Holy Spirit guides our speech in this way, we are piloted by God Himself.

6. THE TONGUE IS A FIRE: Fire spreads rapidly, destroying everything in its path, and words can have the same effect. Just consider how fast gossip spreads and what destructive effect it can have on the lives of others. Fire can also burn the one who wields it in the same way our own words can damage our lives.

IT IS SET ON FIRE BY HELL: God used the Word to create the universe, but Satan perverted the power of words when he seduced Eve to eat the forbidden fruit. The evil one continues to use words today to lead people away from God, and Christians must be constantly on guard against the dangerous force of the tongue.

8. NO MAN CAN TAME THE TONGUE: This would be bad news for us if the story ended here. What good would James' admonitions do concerning the tongue if we were powerless to control it? But Christians have the Holy Spirit living within them, and it is through His power that they can truly tame the tongue.

9. WE CURSE MEN: James emphasized throughout his letter that Christians must treat other people with gentleness and respect, for to do otherwise is hypocrisy. Mankind was created in the image of God (see Genesis 1:26–27), so everyone we meet bears God's imprint (similitude). How can we bless God with one breath but then curse those who bear His image with the next? God calls us to be consistent with our speech—consistently godly.

11–12. SPRING . . . FIG TREE . . . GRAPEVINE: These three illustrations from nature demonstrate the sinfulness of cursing.

UNLEASHING THE TEXT

1) What does it mean that the adulteress's lips "drip honey" and her mouth is "smoother than oil" (Proverbs 5:3)? How is this different from the wise person's speech?

_____

_____

_____

2) What kind of speaker "winks with the eye" (Proverbs 10:10)? What does this mean? How can we detect such motives in another person?

_____

_____

_____

3) Where does understanding come from? Why is it important in our speech?

_____

_____

_____

4) When have you seen someone use knowledge rightly? When have you seen someone use it wrongly? What constitutes a right use of knowledge versus a wrong use?

_____

_____

_____

EXPLORING THE MEANING

Our words affect our actions and the actions of others. Life seems to be filled with talk. The media bombards us with words, politicians prate ceaselessly about the economy and social affairs, and people debate their opinions about everything under the sun. "It's all just words," we say, implying that words without action have no meaning.

But the Bible teaches us that our words have a powerful effect, both on ourselves and on others. James used the illustration of a wildfire to indicate the destruction that can be caused by idle or careless speech. It can burn the person who utters it and scald the person who hears it. It can also spread its destruction in a wide circle as one person's words are repeated by another. Each speaker's utterances lead to actions by himself or those around him.

However, this principle can also work in a positive way. As we learn to speak words of wisdom, we increase the likelihood that we will act in wisdom and encourage others to live in godliness. Consider James's analogy of a ship under the power of the wind: the pilot guides the rudder, and the rudder steers the ship. When we submit to the guidance of the Holy Spirit, He guides us in the use of our tongues, and our tongues can steer us into Christlike character.

Speak the truth in love. The world teaches that we should speak our minds freely, without regard to the effects our words may have on others. Indeed, according to the world's wisdom, people can become "repressed" or "inhibited" if they try to bottle up their thoughts and passions. Therefore, say the experts, it is healthy to be a "straight shooter" and give free vent to every opinion—even (and usually) negative opinions and criticism.

Yet this is not how God wants His children to use their tongues. James exhorts us to "be swift to hear, slow to speak, slow to wrath; for the wrath of man does not produce the righteousness of God" (1:19–20). God's repeatedly commands us to speak the truth—but to do so in a gentle and loving spirit (see Ephesians 4:15). As Proverbs makes clear, lies and deception should never be found on the tongues of God's people. All our speech should be seasoned with knowledge and gentleness.

No one wants to be lied to, and no one enjoys harsh criticism—even if the criticism is true. We strengthen the body of Christ when we speak the truth in love. "Therefore, putting away lying, 'Let each one of you speak truth with his neighbor,' for we are members of one another . . . Let no corrupt word proceed out of your mouth, but what is good for necessary edification, that it may impart grace to the hearers" (Ephesians 4:25, 29).

Wise speech grows from the storehouse of Scripture. One of the things that distinguish the wise speaker from the fool is that he or she "uses knowledge rightly, but the mouth of fools pours forth foolishness" (Proverbs 15:2). The reason for this is simple: the fool has no knowledge of the things of God. Indeed, "the fool has said in his heart, 'There *is* no God'" (Psalm 14:1, emphasis added).

We do well to remember, however, that we are all fools by nature. As Proverbs declares, "foolishness is bound up in the heart of a child" (Proverbs 22:15). It is in the nature of all people to turn away from God and pursue folly, and it is only through the Holy Spirit and the Word of God that anyone can hope to gain knowledge and understanding.

Those who wish to grow in wisdom must store up knowledge in much the same way one stores grain in a warehouse or puts money in the bank. Our storehouse is built on Scripture, and deposits are made through personal and corporate study of God's Word. Wise behavior grows out of wise words, and wise words grow out of our knowledge of God's character. The more we study the Bible and know it in our heart, the more our conversation will be seasoned with knowledge and understanding.

Reflecting on the Text

5) What does it mean when we say that "love covers all sins" (Proverbs 10:12)? When have you experienced this? How is this balanced with speaking the truth?

_____

_____

_____

_____

6) When have you seen a soft answer turn away wrath (see Proverbs 15:1)? When have you seen inflammatory speech stir up wrath? How does one gain the skill of defusing anger?

_____

_____

_____

7) What did James mean when he said the tongue "is set on fire by hell" (James 3:6)? When have you experienced this yourself? What is the cure?

_____

_____

_____

8) If no one can tame the tongue (see James 3:8), then what hope is there of gaining control over it? What role does God play in this? What role do we play?

_____

_____

_____

PERSONAL RESPONSE

9) What influence do your words generally have in the lives of others? In your own life? How can the Holy Spirit help you improve in this area?

_____

_____

_____

10) How well stocked is your storehouse of knowledge? How can you increase
its contents?

_____

_____

_____

6

ACTING WITH WISDOM
Proverbs 6:6–11; 10:1–9; 12:11–28; 21:5–31; 26:13–17

DRAWING NEAR

When was a time you were guilty of not acting when you knew you should?
What motivated you to procrastinate and not do that particular task?

_____

_____

_____

THE CONTEXT

The book of Proverbs addresses many areas of fleshly behavior, both warning
against the dangers and admonishing the reader to instead pursue godliness
and wisdom. Solomon and the others who contributed to this book used cari-
catures, small word portraits of people who are controlled by carnal desires, to
caution against living life according to the flesh.

One such caricature is that of the *sluggard:* a lazy person who indulges
his fleshly desire for rest and pleasure. The sluggard does not like to work but
prefers to sleep long hours and eat gourmet meals. When he does work, he
performs only the barest minimum needed to attain his more immediate goal:
more rest and relaxation. Ironically, the sluggard simultaneously expends great

creative energy in his pursuit of leisure time, dreaming up the most outlandish excuses to avoid work. The sluggard does not act in wisdom.

The principles in this study are aimed primarily at the sin of sloth, but they apply just as well to any area of fleshly excess. The Lord wants His children to mortify the flesh, put to death the passions that lead to destruction, and cultivate the fruit of the Spirit. For the sluggard, this means throwing off the bedclothes and getting busy with the work God has provided.

KEYS TO THE TEXT

Read Proverbs 6:6–11, noting the key words and phrases indicated below.

GO TO THE ANT: The authors of Proverbs frequently consider the lower orders of creation to help their readers understand spiritual principles. One such creature is the ant.

6:6. GO TO THE ANT: The ant provides a picture of industry and self-motivation—a stark contrast to a sluggard. The sluggard is a lazy person with no self-control who uses his energies and resources to find excuses to avoid work.

7. NO CAPTAIN, OVERSEER OR RULER: The ant does not need to be commanded to work; neither does it have to be supervised to ensure that it carries out its responsibilities correctly. In these verses, the contrast with the sluggard is implied—while the ant needs no supervisor, the sluggard must be driven to work by someone else.

8. PROVIDES HER SUPPLIES IN THE SUMMER, AND GATHERS HER FOOD IN THE HARVEST: The ant looks ahead to the future, laying up stores when work is easy to provide for times when work is scarce. *Summer* and *harvest* refer to those times when work is plentiful and appropriate, anticipating the scarcity of winter, when food will not be available. Such cycles are natural in life, but the lazy person does not look ahead or make provisions for the future.

9. HOW LONG WILL YOU SLUMBER: The authors of Proverbs characterize the sluggard as one who loves to sleep. Of course, there is nothing inherently wrong with rest and relaxation—rest is, after all, just another facet of life's natural cycles. But the lazy person overindulges in sedentary activities. In modern parlance, one might call him a couch potato.

10. A LITTLE SLEEP: The sluggard has a habit of excusing his slothfulness "just this once" and asking for "just a little more." At times we can all relate to the temptation, when the alarm goes off in the dark hours, to indulge in just a few more minutes in bed. However, the sluggard's life is characterized by such thinking.

11. LIKE A PROWLER . . . LIKE AN ARMED MAN: The authors of Proverbs constantly emphasize the fact that laziness leads to poverty. The picture here is that poverty will overpower the lazy person, taking him captive and robbing him like an armed thief. When an armed robber kicks in one's door, it is too late to take precautions against him. Likewise, when the sluggard realizes he is impoverished, it will be too late for him to do anything about it.

Read Proverbs 10:1–9, noting the key words and phrases indicated below.

DIVERGENT PATHS: The course of the fool brings grief to his parents and leads him to destruction. But the way of the righteous brings joy to his mother and father and leads him to blessings.

10:1. A FOOLISH SON IS THE GRIEF OF HIS MOTHER: When a child heeds correction and makes wise choices in life, it brings the parents joy. By contrast, when a fool refuses correction, it brings grief to the parents. This parental grief is perhaps most deeply felt by the mother, who plays a more intimate role in raising the child.

2. RIGHTEOUSNESS DELIVERS FROM DEATH: The sluggard seeks treasures of wickedness that bring no real profit, but the righteous gain the greatest of all treasures—eternal life.

3. DESIRE OF THE WICKED: For a while, the wicked and slothful may seem to realize their desires, but in the end God removes their accomplishments because they are evil.

4. THE HAND OF THE DILIGENT MAKES RICH: The sluggard, by contrast, does nothing and thus falls into poverty. Note that poverty by itself is not evil, unless it is the product of laziness.

5. HE WHO GATHERS IN SUMMER . . . HE WHO SLEEPS IN HARVEST: This echoes the words of Proverbs 6:8. The timing necessary in agriculture can be applied to the general laying hold of life's opportunities.

7. THE MEMORY OF THE RIGHTEOUS IS BLESSED: This refers to the way righteous people—those who are diligent and studious to walk in righteousness—are remembered by others on earth and by God in heaven after their death.

8. THE WISE IN HEART WILL RECEIVE COMMANDS: Wise people listen and are teachable, and as a result they are lifted up. Foolish people, always following their own way, fall because they reject God's commands. To be wise we must be willing to work at following God's commands.

9. HE WHO WALKS WITH INTEGRITY: Those with integrity (who act on what they believe) exist without fear of some evil being discovered, while those who are perverse and have secret wickedness will not be able to hide it forever.

Read Proverbs 12:11–28, noting the key words and phrases indicated below.

THE DILIGENT SHALL RULE: *Laziness leads to enslavement, but the person who works with diligence will rise to roles of leadership— and the sluggard will end up working for him.*

12:11. HE WHO TILLS HIS LAND . . . HE WHO PLOWS FRIVOLITY: The diligent man "tills his land" and pursues whatever labor he finds for his profit. The principle is not dependent on ownership of land but rather describes an attitude toward the work that the diligent man has at hand. The hardworking person does his job faithfully, regardless of what that job might be. The sluggard, by contrast, is not interested in doing his work. He "lives for the weekend," and his focus is continually on the pursuit of pleasure and entertainment. Such people are always on the lookout for get-rich quick schemes.

12. THE WICKED COVET THE CATCH . . . THE RIGHTEOUS YIELDS FRUIT: The wicked desire the treasures gained by the schemes of evil men, but the righteous live simple lives of obedience that produce blessings.

14. FRUIT OF HIS MOUTH: This deals with the power of words—the reward of wise words is like the reward for physical labor.

16. A PRUDENT MAN COVERS SHAME: The prudent man is a model of self-control and ignores an insult. He speaks truth and promotes justice.

18. SPEAKS LIKE THE PIERCINGS OF A SWORD: The contrast here is between cutting words that are spoken "rashly" (Psalm 106:33) and thoughtful words that bring health.

20. DECEIT IS IN THE HEART . . . BUT COUNSELORS OF PEACE HAVE JOY: Those who plan evil by deceit have no joy because of the risks and dangers in their plan. But the righteous who lead by peace fear nothing, and thus have joy.

23. A PRUDENT MAN CONCEALS KNOWELDGE: Again, unlike the fool who makes everyone hear his folly, the wise person is a model of restraint and humility, speaking what he knows at an appropriate time.

24. THE HAND OF THE DILIGENT WILL RULE . . . THE LAZY MAN WILL BE PUT TO FORCED LABOR: Those who are self-motivated and industrious invariably rise to positions of authority over those who are not. Unlike the ant, which was pictured earlier as a creature that requires no overseer, the sluggard will not work unless he is driven by others. The lazy man needs an overseer, who is pictured here as a slave driver.

26. THE WAY OF THE WICKED: This verse could be understood as saying that the righteous person guides his friends carefully, unlike the wicked person who leads his companions astray. As Paul would later write, "Do not be deceived: 'Evil company corrupts good habits'" (1 Corinthians 15:33).

27. WHAT HE TOOK IN HUNTING . . . DILIGENCE IS MAN'S PRECIOUS POSSESSION: It is interesting that the sluggard is shown here as actually working and making the effort to go out hunting for his food. But the implication is that he was probably forced to do it. Once the overseer's whip is removed, the sluggard reverts to his natural ways, too indolent even to roast his own food. So, while he might actually work sometimes, he rarely finishes what he starts. The wise man knows diligence is a precious treasure that a person should strive to attain.

Read Proverbs 21:5–31, noting the key words and phrases indicated below.

GET-RICH-QUICK SCHEMES: The sluggard desires wealth as much as anyone—he just doesn't want to work for it. His conflicting desires will destroy him.

21:5. EVERYONE WHO IS HASTY: The contrast here is between the diligent, who carefully plan ahead, and the sluggard, who hopes to get rich quickly and with little investment. The diligent worker makes a concerted effort at every step of a project, striving to do his best and produce quality work. The sluggard, on the other hand, maintains a "good enough" work ethic.

9. BETTER TO DWELL IN A CORNER OF A HOUSETOP: Roofs in biblical times were open-like patios, so a small arbor or enclosure in the corner of a flat roof was an inconvenient place to live.

10. WICKED DESIRES EVIL: So strongly does the wicked person seek to do evil that he will not spare his neighbor if he gets in his way.

13. SHUTS HIS EARS TO THE CRY OF THE POOR: It offends the Creator when a person neglects the poor, who are part of His creation.

17. HE WHO LOVES PLEASURE: When the sluggard does work, his motivation is to attain pleasure. The diligent, by contrast, work with a long-term perspective. Wine and oil suggest luxury and self-indulgence—things the diligent avoid but the sluggard craves.

25. THE DESIRE OF THE LAZY MAN KILLS HIM: The sluggard often has expensive tastes, and he covets the lifestyle of the rich and famous. The problem is that he is unwilling to expend long-term effort in acquiring the resources to live in high style even if such a goal were worthwhile. (Proverbs makes it abundantly clear that such a goal leads a man to destruction.)

26. THE RIGHTEOUS GIVES AND DOES NOT SPARE: The wise person is not focused on such temporal riches and luxuries but on eternal treasure. This focus enables the wise to give to the poor rather than consuming his wealth on dissipation and pleasure.

Read Proverbs 26:13–17, noting the key words and phrases indicated below.

THE RUSTY HINGE: The lazy man expends a great deal of energy finding excuses to avoid working. His problem is that he is wise in his own eyes.

26:13. THERE IS A LION IN THE ROAD: The authors of Proverbs frequently make fun of the sluggard by using humor to underscore the extent to which a lazy person will go to avoid work—even to the point of inventing ludicrous excuses. The effort involved in avoiding work is scarcely less than what would be required to get up and do it!

14. AS A DOOR TURNS ON ITS HINGES: Here is another humorous portrait of the sluggard. One can picture him swinging from side to side, as securely attached to his bed as a door is to its frame.

15. BURIES HIS HAND IN THE BOWL: The sluggard is often made weaker by wealth. This man has food in his bowl, making it unnecessary (for the moment) to get up and find something to eat. Yet even in this good fortune, he is too lazy to feed himself what he has.

16. WISER IN HIS OWN EYES: To be wise in one's own eyes is a grave danger. "Do you see a man wise in his own eyes? There is more hope for a fool than for him" (Proverbs 26:12). The solution to this danger is to recognize there is no true wisdom apart from God. "Do not be wise in your own eyes; fear the LORD and depart from evil. It will be health to your flesh, and strength to your bones" (3:7–8).

GOING DEEPER

Read 2 Thessalonians 3:10–15, noting the key words and phrases indicated below.

> AVOID THE SLUGGARD: *Paul takes a strong stand against the sin of sloth, warning that those who don't work shouldn't eat. He calls Christians to hold one another accountable.*

3:10. IF ANYONE WILL NOT WORK: Paul wrote this epistle to the Christians in Thessalonica to address a number of specific issues, one of which was that some of the believers there were not working for a living. Much of the letter concerns the return of Christ, and it is possible some believers were using hope for the rapture as an excuse to avoid work. Note that Paul spoke of those who *won't* work, as opposed to those who *can't* work for some legitimate reason.

NEITHER SHALL HE EAT: Paul's basic premise is simple: if you want to eat, you'll have to work. This principle does not preclude Christian charity; rather, it counterbalances it. Christians are commanded to share their blessings with others, but those who receive are also commanded to be diligent in whatever work the Lord has made available to them.

11. A DISORDERLY MANNER: The Greek word translated *disorderly* was used to describe soldiers who had stepped out of rank in marching formation. Those who refuse to work for a living are refusing to follow the prescribed rule and declining to fulfill their own natural obligations.

BUT ARE BUSYBODIES: The sluggard has too much time on his hands, and he fills it with destructive pursuits. Those who have no affairs of their own to attend to inevitably begin to meddle in the affairs of others.

12. WORK IN QUIETNESS: It is an interesting paradox that when the sluggard does find work to do, he generally makes a big show of being busy. The cure for gossip and interference is to be busy with one's own work.

EAT THEIR OWN BREAD: Paul commanded the Thessalonians not to live on handouts and charity but to meet their own basic needs.

13. DO NOT GROW WEARY IN DOING GOOD: This is the most important work for God's people: to be diligent in doing good. This involves first meeting one's own obligations and then sharing the Lord's blessings with others.

14. DO NOT KEEP COMPANY WITH HIM: Paul commanded the Thessalonian believers not to be socially involved with sluggards. This withdrawal of companionship was intended to force the idle to meet their own needs rather than relying on the pity of others. The goal was for them to "be ashamed" and therefore repent of their disobedience to God's commands.

16. ADMONISH HIM AS A BROTHER: Paul did not intend this withdrawal of companionship to be a punishment but an admonishment. *Admonish* literally means "to advise toward," or in other words, to counsel, warn, or remind a person of his duties. The goal was to remind those who refused to work that they had an obligation to do so. They were not enemies of the Christians but merely brothers and sisters who needed some correction. Paul was directing the Thessalonians to hate the sin but love the sinner.

UNLEASHING THE TEXT

1) In what ways does an ant differ from a lazy person? What other creatures demonstrate diligence and industry?

_____

_____

_____

_____

2) What motivates a person to be lazy? What motivates a person to be diligent and industrious? How can we cultivate diligence and avoid sloth?

_____

_____

_____

3) What does it mean to "follow frivolity" (Proverbs 12:11)? Give specific examples. What is the opposite of this behavior?

_____

_____

_____

4) What does it mean to be hasty? How is this also consistent with being lazy? What motivates a person to be this way?

_____

_____

_____

_____

EXPLORING THE MEANING

Christians should work for a living. The sluggard hasn't got the energy to do any work, although, ironically, he does have the energy to contrive outlandish excuses to avoid it. He also tends to enjoy the finer things in life, appreciating luxury and fine dining—preferably at someone else's expense. Any work that he does perform is done halfheartedly, with the expectation of a generous paycheck while not concerning himself in the least with the quality of his work.

God's people should not live this way. The satisfaction that comes from working hard is one of the gifts of grace that God gives men. "Nothing is better for a man than that he should eat and drink, and that his soul should enjoy good in his labor" (Ecclesiastes 2:24). God made people for a task, and when they work hard at that task, they not only provide for their families but also bring glory to God.

Paul laid out the principle in simple terms: he who does not work does not eat. This does not provide an excuse for Christians to turn a blind eye to those who are in need. It does, however, demand accountability from those who refuse to work, especially when they have the ability and opportunity to do so. Meeting one's basic needs is a Christian's duty.

The love of money is a sin. The sluggard may work hard to avoid work, but when he's got work, he doesn't like to work hard at doing it. Wealth is always appealing, but the effort required to gain it is not. Consequently, the sluggard is easily susceptible to the sin of loving money.

Paul writes that "the love of money is a root of all kinds of evil" (1 Timothy 6:10). This is because it causes people to become more obsessed with the things of this world and less passionate about the things of God. When people love money, they become stingy and close their hand to the poor. They make decisions based on finances rather than on God's will. They forget that the riches this world offers are of no value in eternity. This is why Jesus said, "You cannot serve both God and money" (Luke 16:13 NIV).

This principle also applies to the daily work that the Lord has provided for each of us. A job is a gift from the Lord, and it is also a ministry that He expects us to perform to the best of our abilities—working as unto Him, not our earthly masters (see Ephesians 6:5–8). As Solomon reminds us, "Whatever your hand finds to do, do it with your might; for there is no work or device or knowledge or wisdom in the grave where you are going" (Ecclesiastes 9:10).

Laziness leads to personal destruction. The sluggard has an excessive love for rest and relaxation. Again, these things in themselves are not sinful—the sin comes when leisure pursuits become a consuming passion. The person who sleeps or plays when he should be working will be overtaken by poverty, and it will come on him unexpectedly and irresistibly like an armed robber. The individual with too much time on his hands will also find things to do with that time that will cause harm to himself and to others, such as becoming a busybody who meddles in affairs that are none of his business.

This principle, of course, is not limited to laziness; it holds true for any fleshly passion we allow to rule our lives. The sin of laziness is just one of many ways that Christians can permit their flesh to govern their lives, and the result is always crippling. As Paul confessed, "I know that in me [that is, in my flesh] nothing good dwells; for to will is present with me, but how to perform what is good I do not find . . . O wretched man that I am! Who will deliver me from this body of death?" (Romans 7:18, 24).

The answer to this question is Jesus Christ—it is He who delivers us from the body of sin and from the eternal destruction that would otherwise be our fate. Thanks to Him, we have the power and presence of the Holy Spirit working in our lives, and He gives us the ability to subdue the flesh and obey His Word. And we *need* that. The ways of the flesh lead to destruction, but the ways of God lead to wisdom and eternal life.

REFLECTING ON THE TEXT

5) What does it mean to be wise in one's own eyes? How does a person become this way? Why is it dangerous? What is the antidote?

_____

_____

_____

_____

6) Why did Paul decree that anyone who did not work should not eat? How do we balance this with the Lord's commands to care for the needy?

_____

_____

_____

7) In what ways is a sluggard disorderly? What does this mean in practical terms? What is required of Christians if we are to be orderly?

_____

_____

_____

8) What does it mean to admonish another Christian? How is this done? When is it required? How does one balance this with not being a meddler or a busybody?

_____

_____

_____

PERSONAL RESPONSE

9) How diligent are you in doing the work the Lord has given you? In your job? In your ministries? In your family life?

_____

_____

_____

10) Is there an area of fleshly passion that is struggling for control in your life? How can you gain victory through God's Word? Through the power of the Holy Spirit?

_____

_____

_____

7

PERSEVERING IN WISDOM
Proverbs 1:20–33; 3:1–35

DRAWING NEAR

When was a time in your life that you gave up doing something but later wished you had stuck with it? What did you learn from that experience?

_____

_____

_____

THE CONTEXT

Solomon was the wisest man who ever lived, yet something happened along the way that caused him to stop persevering in wisdom. Instead of continuing along the path of righteousness, he resorted to walking according to the flesh. This begs the question: *If the wisest man of all time did not finish strong, how can we hope to do any better?*

The truth is that wisdom is not a one-time acquisition but a daily commitment to walk according to the Word of God. Solomon did not finish strong because he neglected God's Word, and when someone strays from that course, he will inevitably stray from wisdom. Finishing strong requires daily *application* of God's Word to our lives. Biblical wisdom is practical, so it can be seen in daily decisions and a person's lifestyle. It is not merely a collection of knowledge.

If the Christian life is a "race that is set before us" (Hebrews 12:1), then finishing strong is key. When we become Christians, we are not miraculously transported to heaven but are left on earth to fight the fight of faith and run the race laid out before us. We achieve endurance when we submit our lives to the teachings of God's Word and seek to apply those teachings through the power of the Holy Spirit. When we submit to the Spirit, He shows us the areas in which we need to strengthen our walk and purify our lives—and He gives us the power to do it.

This process involves more discipline than a normal race, but the stakes are much greater. As Paul said, "Do you not know that those who run in a race all run, but one receives the prize? . . . Now they do it to obtain a perishable crown, but we for an imperishable crown" (1 Corinthians 9:24–25). When we rely on the Spirit of God to help us fight sin and grow in grace, we will be enabled to finish the race—and finish strong.

KEYS TO THE TEXT

Read Proverbs 1:20–33, noting the key words and phrases indicated below.

> WISDOM CALLS OUT TO THE SIMPLE: *Wisdom is personified as a woman standing in the public square and calling out to the people passing by.*

1:20. WISDOM CALLS ALOUD OUTSIDE: Wisdom calls aloud in the public square, suggesting that knowledge of God and wisdom to live according to His principles are readily available to anyone who seeks them. Wisdom is not restricted to those with education or a good background or any other attribute—it is a free gift of God, given to any who request it (see James 1:5).

23. TURN AT MY REBUKE: To turn is to repent. It is to recognize one is heading in the wrong direction and rotate 180 degrees to go the opposite way. The writers of Proverbs place great importance on the ability to accept a rebuke—it is one of the things that distinguish the wise man from the fool. The

wise person will hear a judicious rebuke, examine his ways to see where he has strayed from God's path, and turn back to the right way.

I WILL POUR OUT MY SPIRIT ON YOU: True wisdom comes from God alone, and He is eager to pour it forth through His Spirit into our lives. But to receive that outpouring, we must obey what He has revealed to us. Wisdom grows through practical application as we obey God.

24. I HAVE CALLED . . . I HAVE STRETCHED OUT MY HAND: Wisdom is the one who always takes the initiative, reaching out to those who need her. It is God who makes the overtures to humanity, offering us salvation and wisdom as free gifts—but it is up to us to accept those gifts.

THE FATE OF THOSE WHO REFUSE: Wisdom warns her hearers there are dire consequences for ignoring her free offer.

25. WOULD HAVE NONE OF MY REBUKE: David sinned against God but repented when he was rebuked. His willingness to accept correction enabled him to finish his life well and be called a man after God's own heart (see Acts 13:22). In contrast, Solomon did not heed the Lord's rebuke but continued obstinately in his sinful ways—and he did not finish the race as he had begun.

26. I ALSO WILL LAUGH AT YOUR CALAMITY: Every person has a conscience that convicts him or her of sin and points to the truth of the gospel. Yet people reject those warnings and spend their lives taking good things from God without thanks—all the while speaking wickedly of Him and refusing to submit to His authority. When the day of judgment comes, those who have rejected God's wisdom may call on Him for relief, but their cries will be met with derision.

29. THEY HATED KNOWLEDGE: Those who reject the knowledge of God demonstrate hatred for knowledge—even though they may think they are knowledgeable and enjoy learning. The only knowledge that counts for eternity is knowledge of God.

30. DESPISED MY EVERY REBUKE: God's rebukes are vital because they are designed to keep us close to Him and walking in the paths of wisdom and righteousness. They are not the harsh punishments of a slave master but the gentle reproofs of a teacher who wants a pupil to excel. The person who finishes well listens carefully to the rebukes of wisdom.

31. THEY SHALL EAT THE FRUIT OF THEIR OWN WAY: The Bible makes it clear we reap what we sow (see Galatians 6:7). The fool insists on sowing seeds of folly, so he inevitably eats its fruits.

32. THE COMPLACENCY OF FOOLS WILL DESTROY THEM: Complacency is a deadly sin, as it numbs a person to the promptings of the Holy Spirit. The complacent Christian is like a runner who gains ground in a race only to sit down in the shade and take a nap. We must keep moving forward and follow the Word of God through the leadership of the Holy Spirit if we want to finish the race admirably.

33. WHOEVER LISTENS TO ME WILL DWELL SAFELY: The good news in this is that God does not abandon His children or leave us to finish the race in our own power. He is constantly at work to keep us on the right path, strengthening our character and faith to become more like Christ. Anyone who listens to the teachings of God will run the race effectively.

Read Proverbs 3:1–35, noting the key words and phrases indicated below.

> REMEMBER GOD'S LAW: *Wisdom does not guarantee that a person will finish the race well, as Solomon's life demonstrates. We must take care not to forget God's Word.*

3:1. DO NOT FORGET MY LAW: Here again we are reminded that we must make a diligent effort to put God's law into practice by studying it and meditating on it regularly. If we do not maintain our daily diet of God's Word, we run the danger of forgetting His law.

2. LENGTH OF DAYS AND LONG LIFE AND PEACE: These are among the temporal blessings that wisdom bestows. Solomon did not enjoy these benefits but finished his days earlier than he might have otherwise, amid great turmoil in his kingdom.

3. AROUND YOUR NECK . . . TABLET OF YOUR HEART: Wisdom is both internal and external. We incorporate it into our lives as we store up knowledge in our hearts through God's Word, and then we apply it outwardly in obedience. The outward manifestation of wisdom causes a wise person to find favor in the eyes of man, while God is pleased to look on the wise person's heart.

5. WITH ALL YOUR HEART: The Lord said, "Judah has not turned to Me with her whole heart, but in pretense" (Jeremiah 3:10). This suggests we can make an outward show of devotion to God while still setting up idols in our hearts. If we want to finish the race well, we must allow the Lord to root out such pretenses and create in us a whole heart devoted solely to Him.

LEAN NOT ON YOUR OWN UNDERSTANDING: In other words, we should not depend on our earthly wisdom to understand what God is doing. The word *lean* means "support yourself," suggesting a person can depend on his own fleshly perspective to find wisdom—but this leads only to sin and folly.

PRACTICAL WISDOM: Solomon offers advice on how to put wisdom into daily practice. As we honor the Lord, He will guide our paths.

6. IN ALL YOUR WAYS ACKNOWLEDGE HIM: That is, we deliberately remind ourselves that God is absolutely sovereign over all the affairs of our life and is in control of every circumstance. As we acknowledge His lordship in our daily lives, we will grow to serve Him in all things.

HE SHALL DIRECT YOUR PATHS: This can often include hardship and suffering, as well as prosperity and pleasure. But when we remember to acknowledge God's sovereign hand, we will be able to trust He is leading us down the best possible path.

7. DO NOT BE WISE IN YOUR OWN EYES: A person who is wise in his own eyes is depending on fleshly wisdom, the wisdom from below, to deal with the circumstances of life. The humble person, by contrast, recognizes that all true wisdom comes from above, from God alone, and he asks faithfully for God to grant him wisdom.

FEAR THE LORD AND DEPART FROM EVIL: These two things go hand in hand. "Fear of the Lord" is a deep respect for His authority, which leads to obedience to His commands. Wisdom is practical; it must be put into practice to become true wisdom—it is not mere head knowledge.

9. HONOR THE LORD WITH YOUR POSSESSIONS: WE must remember that everything we have is a gift from God, including all we possess. God wants us to use His gifts in His service to others, not in selfish pursuits. This includes regular tithing, giving Him the "firstfruits" of all our increase, and

not selfishly hoarding our possessions but generously using them in His service.

> *DO NOT DESPISE CORRECTION: Wisdom is an active process,*
> *and there are times when we all must be chastised. The wise man*
> *does not fight against God's correction.*

11. DO NOT DESPISE THE CHASTENING OF THE LORD: Once again, we are reminded of the importance of the Lord's correction. The wise man accepts correction, remembering he is sinful and imperfect, whereas the fool despises correction and remains wise in his own eyes.

12. WHOM THE LORD LOVES HE CORRECTS: God's hand of discipline is not cruel and arbitrary but loving and gentle. His rebukes are always intended to help us grow stronger. He does not delight in pointing out our shortcomings but in seeing us become more like Christ.

19. THE LORD BY WISDOM FOUNDED THE EARTH: The Bible tells us that Jesus was the agent of creation (see John 1:1–3). As we increase in wisdom, we become more like Christ and gain more wisdom by imitating Him continually.

21. LET THEM NOT DEPART FROM YOUR EYES: By keeping our eyes on Christ and imitating Him in all we do and say, we will steadily attain wisdom from above.

25. TROUBLE . . . WHEN IT COMES: Solomon acknowledged that everyone—even the wise—will face troubled times. The wise man is distinguished from the fool in the way he responds to trouble when it comes. The fool races about in fear and panic, depending on his earthly wisdom to deal with the crisis, while the wise man reminds himself that God is sovereign.

27. DO NOT WITHOLD GOOD: The truly wise person learns to love others as he loves himself, humbly considering others as better than himself (see Matthew 22:39; Philippians 2:3).

32. THE PERVERSE PERSON: The perverse person does things his own way, disregarding the commands of God. The Lord withholds wisdom from those who refuse to obey Him, but He shares His inmost confidences with those who follow His commands.

35. SHAME SHALL BE THE LEGACY OF FOOLS: Only the wise will finish the race with excellence. Those who persist in going their own way will end their days as fools.

Going Deeper

Read Hebrews 12:1–11, noting the key words and phrases indicated below.

Run the Christian Race: The author of Hebrews gives us some practical advice on how to finish strong. He likens the Christian's life to a race—a long and difficult pursuit.

12:1. WE ARE SURROUNDED BY SO GREAT A CLOUD OF WITNESSES: This refers to the saints described in Hebrews 11. It does not mean the Old Testament saints are watching us like spectators at a race. Rather, their lives provide examples and testimonies to help us understand how to run the race with diligence.

LAY ASIDE EVERY WEIGHT: No runner would dream of wearing combat boots or carrying a backpack filled with toys. In the same way, we must be on guard to prevent the things of life from becoming a burden—possessions, temporal pursuits, leisure activities, and so forth.

THE SIN WHICH SO EASILY ENSNARES: The image here is of a marathon runner going cross-country and not running on a cultivated track. There are countless things to trip on when running through the countryside, so the athlete keeps an eye on the path in front of him. The same principle holds true for the believer: we must be constantly examining our path, watching for those sins and temptations that threaten to make us fall.

RUN WITH ENDURANCE: The Christian life is a marathon, not a short sprint. Wisdom requires daily maintenance—a regular diet of Scripture reading, prayer, and obedience. The Greek word translated *race* is the root of our English word *agony*. The implication is that endurance requires hard work and sometimes even prolonged times of suffering and hardship. We must not give up on our walk with Christ if we intend to finish the race well.

2. THE AUTHOR AND FINISHER OF OUR FAITH: Jesus is the author of our faith because it is through Him that salvation is possible. He is the paramount example of what it means to walk in wisdom. He is also the finisher of our faith, because He is always working to complete in us the fullness of His image. We do not run the race alone or under our own power.

FOR THE JOY THAT WAS SET BEFORE HIM: It seems incongruent that Jesus looked at the cross with joy. This joy did not come *in* the sufferings but *through* the sufferings, as He was then able to make atonement for sin, once and for all.

3. LEST YOU BECOME WEARY AND DISCOURAGED IN YOUR SOULS: Discouragement and despair are the enemies of our souls. Christians must guard against such thinking, keeping in mind what Jesus endured for our sake as He completed the work the Father gave Him. Again, this involves keeping our eyes focused on the eternal rather than on the temporal.

11. NO CHASTENING SEEMS TO BE JOYFUL FOR THE PRESENT: Here is the core of finishing strong: the resolve to accept chastening as from God, recognizing it is intended to strengthen our souls.

UNLEASHING THE TEXT

1) Why does Solomon depict wisdom standing in the public square, calling to passersby (see Proverbs 1:20)? What does this teach about wisdom? About human nature?

_____

_____

_____

2) What role does chastisement play in gaining wisdom? In keeping wisdom? Why is it important?

_____

_____

_____

3) In what ways is wisdom both internal and external? How do we incorporate wisdom into our hearts and our minds? What results will we see when we do this?

_____

_____

_____

4) Why must we accept God's chastening if we want to be wise? What benefits does it bring to our lives?

_____

_____

_____

_____

Exploring the Meaning

We must take care not to forget God's Word. Proverbs teaches us that knowledge of God's Word is essential if we are to gain wisdom. Yet it also reminds us that we can easily forget God's Word, which will cause us to stray from the paths of wisdom into any number of foolish pursuits. This was precisely what happened to Solomon. Although God had granted him immense wisdom in his young adulthood, he gradually forgot the very commands the Lord had given him concerning pagan practices.

We run the danger of forgetting God's Word when we fail to obey and apply it to our lives. We increase our knowledge by spending time in private study of the Bible and through corporate times of worship and teaching. Beyond this, it is imperative that we remember wisdom is very practical: it must be used if it is to flourish. We use our wisdom when we obey God's commands, which helps us see the world as God sees it—which is, of course, the ultimate measure of wisdom.

When we understand God's Word but fail to obey it, we are like the person who looks into a mirror and then forgets what he sees. The mirror ceases to be of any practical value to us because we did not adjust our appearance based on what we saw. The book of James reminds us, "If anyone is a hearer of the word and not a doer, he is like a man observing his natural face in a mirror; for he observes himself, goes away, and immediately forgets what kind of man he was. But he who looks into the perfect law of liberty and continues in it, and is not a forgetful hearer but a doer of the work, this one will be blessed in what he does" (1:23–25).

The Lord uses rebuke and correction to keep us running the race. Nobody likes to be criticized, and it can be painful to be reprimanded. Even basic correction can be difficult to endure, especially when it is done in a harsh or demeaning manner. We have all encountered people in our lives who seem to delight in finding fault with others, and it can be hard to see any value in such constant words of criticism. Yet every athlete understands the importance of criticism. Criticism exposes weakness, which, when corrected, makes the athlete perform better. If an athlete ignores his coach, he is only hurting his own performance.

The same principle holds true in the Christian life. None of us is perfect, and we all fall short of the completed image of Christ. Like the athlete, we all have areas that need to be strengthened, and our sinful nature is constantly fighting to reassert itself—even in areas where we've gained victory in the past. This is why it is so important for us to receive the Lord's corrections with a teachable spirit. As Jesus stated, "As many as I love, I rebuke and chasten. Therefore be zealous and repent" (Revelation 3:19).

We do not run the race alone or under our own power. The world of athletic competition features some amazing accomplishments. Runners set world records for speed, mountain climbers demonstrate incredible endurance, skydivers defy death by leaping from great heights—there are countless feats of prowess being undertaken by daring men and women all over the world every day. But there is one thing that all these feats have in common: they are within the realm of possibility for human endeavor.

That is not the case when it comes to the Christian race. We are called to be like Christ, but there is no person on earth who can accomplish that feat in his or her own power. We are all born under the curse of sin, and none of us can overcome that curse. Left to our own devices, we could never hope to live as Christ lived, for He was without sin. Thank God we are not left to our own devices! God has given His Spirit to each believer—the very same Spirit that raised Christ from the dead (see Romans 8:1). It is through the power and guidance of the Holy Spirit that we overcome the sinful nature that holds us captive.

Paul once cried, "Oh, what a miserable person I am! Who will free me from this life that is dominated by death?" But no sooner had he uttered this lament than the answer came to him: "Thank God! The answer is in Jesus Christ our Lord" (Romans 7:24–25 NLT). We are called on to endure, to persevere in the race to the end, that we might attain the prize that never fades away—but we are also empowered *by* God Himself to accomplish this task. As long as we remain open to His correction, He will enable us to finish strong.

REFLECTING ON THE TEXT

5) How does a person forget God's law? How did this happen in Solomon's life? How does a Christian guard against this?

_____

_____

_____

6) What does it mean to acknowledge God in all our ways? How is this done? Why is it critical in the life of a Christian?

_____

_____

_____

_____

7) What does it mean to be wise in our own eyes? Give practical examples of this. How does it happen? How can one guard against it?

_____

_____

_____

_____

8) When have you benefited from criticism? In what ways was that criticism unpleasant to hear? What was required of you to submit to it?

_____

_____

_____

PERSONAL RESPONSE

9) What are you doing on a regular basis to ensure you don't forget God's law? How can you improve your storehouse of knowledge?

_____

_____

_____

10) Is the Lord calling you to correct some area of your Christian walk? If so, what will you do this week to address that area?

_____

_____

_____

8

TRUE WISDOM FROM GOD

Proverbs 1:7–19; 14:6–15; 26:7–12

DRAWING NEAR

In what ways have your friends influenced you for good or bad in the past?
How have you been a positive and godly influence to others?

THE CONTEXT

So far in this study, we have examined many aspects of wisdom and folly, and
we have seen the results of each. The difference between wisdom and folly is
so striking and so self-evident that one must wonder why anyone would ever
choose to be a fool. What could possibly make someone lead a life marked by
foolishness?

The answer is actually quite simple: we are all born foolish. True wisdom
comes only from God, but every human being is born into sin, separated from
God, and devoid of wisdom. The only way for anyone to escape folly and find
wisdom is to receive God's forgiveness through the gospel. This brings us into
a relationship with the source of wisdom, and the Holy Spirit then begins His
work of transforming our lives.

But the world does not acknowledge God as the source of true wisdom, for it has its own form of so-called wisdom to lull the simple into complacency. This false wisdom is a mere counterfeit of God's truth, yet on the surface it can seem like sound counsel to those who lack understanding. This is a deadly deception. The sad truth is that even God's people can sometimes be fooled into embracing this kind of false wisdom.

The source of this worldly wisdom is the devil and his demons, and its purpose is to draw people away from following the one true God. Believers must be aware of the two types of wisdom—that from below and that from above—and be able to discern between them. This is the focus of today's study.

Keys to the Text

Read Proverbs 1:7–19, noting the key words and phrases indicated below.

THE BEGINNING OF WISDOM: Before a person can hope to gain wisdom, he or she must first learn a deep reverence for God, because only He is the source of all genuine wisdom.

7. THE FEAR OF THE LORD IS THE BEGINNING OF KNOWLEDGE: Here is a short summary of all that we have been studying concerning wisdom. God is the sole source of true wisdom, and wisdom can be attained only when one holds Him in reverence as Lord and Savior. The overarching theme of Proverbs is this kind of reverence for God, which is foundational for all spiritual knowledge and wisdom. While unbelievers may make statements about life and truth, they do not have true or ultimate knowledge until they are in a redemptive relationship of reverential awe with God.

FOOLS DESPISE WISDOM AND INSTRUCTION: "The fool has said in his heart, 'There is no God'" (Psalm 14:1)—and has cut himself off from the source of wisdom by doing so. The fool hates knowledge and correction. He is quick to argue (see Proverbs 20:3) and just as quick to express anger (see 29:11). He is complacent (see 1:32) and "trusts in his own heart" (28:26). All of these things represent the wisdom of the world.

10. MY SON: Once again, we find the authors of Proverbs using the motif of a wise father instructing his son in the ways of wisdom. The warning to the

"son" here is about the enticement of sinners, who will succeed if the son fails to embrace true wisdom.

IF SINNERS ENTICE YOU: The word translated *entice* means literally "to be open-minded, simple, gullible." The world works overtime to seduce our minds into gullibility, so we must remain keenly aware that Satan is always trying to seduce us away from God. The world system offers what appears to be wisdom on the surface but is actually pseudo-wisdom. Worse, this "wisdom" is not a passive thing, like a choice between different brands in the grocery store. Rather, it is active and used by the enemy of our souls to lead us astray.

> STREET GANG: *Solomon gives us another vignette, this time of criminals enticing a youth to join them. He uses an extreme example to illustrate some common attitudes.*

11. COME WITH US: The fact is that most people follow this invitation and wind up on the wide road to destruction. "For wide is the gate and broad is the way that leads to destruction, and there are many who go in by it" (Matthew 7:13). What these enticers neglect to mention when inviting others to follow is that the source of their wisdom is hell itself.

LET US LIE IN WAIT TO SHED BLOOD: At first reading, Solomon's example of robbery and murder seems extreme. After all, most of us are not invited by friends to go out on a mugging spree, and such an enticement would be easy to resist. But James will show this is exactly what we do when we envy our neighbors and when we set our own interests above the interests of others. The world's wisdom urges us to "look out for number one," but it is actually telling us to "lurk secretly for the innocent without cause."

12. LET US SWALLOW THEM ALIVE: This type of bloodthirsty language seems outrageous to followers of Christ, and they would never believe themselves to be capable of such thinking. Yet James will suggest otherwise. When we follow the wisdom from below, this is precisely the way we end up thinking: other people become mere ends to our means, and we wind up biting and devouring one another.

13. ALL KINDS OF PRECIOUS POSSESSIONS . . . FILL OUR HOUSES WITH SPOIL: The wisdom of this world sets great value on material possessions, social status, leisure time, and so on—values that are constantly touted in our

society today. The wicked enlist the innocent without full disclosure of their intent. They promise abundant spoil through outright robbery, which is made to appear easy and safe for the thieves and murderers.

15. DO NOT WALK IN THE WAY WITH THEM: We must reject sin at the first temptation by refusing even the association that can lead to it. The more we walk in a certain direction, the more we develop a path. Walking on a path implies a consistent lifestyle, but there is only one path that leads to God. The best way to avoid sin is to avoid those people whose paths lead to sin. Christians should not keep company with fools.

17. IN VAIN THE NET IS SPREAD IN THE SIGHT OF ANY BIRD: It would be ineffective for a trapper to set up a net for catching a bird in full view of the bird. In the same way, the sinner must set up his trap for the innocent in secret—but ultimately the trap is sprung on the trapper.

19. GREEDY FOR GAIN: One facet of the wisdom from below is the idea that one must always be gaining more. This is an unattractive quality, and one that puts its possessor on the same level as a grave. "The leech has two daughters—Give and Give! There are three things that are never satisfied, four never say, 'Enough!': The grave, the barren womb, the earth that is not satisfied with water—and the fire never says, 'Enough!'" (Proverbs 30:15–16).

Read Proverbs 14:6–15, noting the key words and phrases indicated below.

LEARN FROM THE FOOL: A wise man can learn wisdom by observing the foolish behavior of the world. But this lesson is best learned from a distance.

14:6. A SCOFFER SEEKS WISDOM: The desire for wisdom is common to all mankind—everyone desires to live with skill, avoid disaster, and find fulfillment. The scoffer cannot find it, however, because he has refused to fear the Lord and has rejected all correction.

KNOWLEDGE IS EASY TO HIM WHO UNDERSTANDS: Understanding is having insight into the character and ways of God; it is the ability to see life from His perspective. This can only come from a personal relationship with God, and that is only available through His Son, Jesus. Those who reject Christ deny themselves of ever finding wisdom.

7. GO FROM THE PRESENCE OF A FOOLISH MAN: Again, Christians are not to keep company with fools. Rather, they are to avoid association with those who cannot teach wisdom.

8. UNDERSTAND HIS WAY: The prudent person pays attention to the path that he is walking, and he learns from words of correction. The fool, by contrast, thinks that he is being prudent when he follows human wisdom, looks after his own interests, and seems wise in his own eyes. This is self-deception.

9. FOOLS MOCK AT SIN: The wisdom embraced by modern society teaches that sin is righteousness and righteousness is sin. The world today mocks the idea that immoral behavior is wrong while simultaneously proclaiming selfishness is a virtue. While fools ridicule their impending judgment, the wise are promised favor with God and man.

10. THE HEART KNOWS ITS OWN BITTERNESS: At its depth, suffering and rejoicing are personal. No one is able to communicate them fully.

12. THERE IS A WAY THAT SEEMS RIGHT TO A MAN: In today's culture, each person does that which is right in his own eyes, but that is the wisdom from below. The wisdom from above dictates that we must do what is right in God's eyes, regardless of what the world may think.

14. BACKSLIDER IN HEART: This term, so often used by the prophets, is used here in such a way as to clarify who is a backslider. He belongs in the category of the fool, the wicked, and the disobedient, and he is contrasted with the godly wise. It is a word that the prophets used of apostate unbelievers.

15. THE SIMPLE BELIEVES EVERY WORD: The world's wisdom is often absurd and even self-contradictory, yet many are still taken in. Fools are gullible because they have rejected the truth; therefore, they readily believe lies. They are like the blind who do not even know what they are stumbling over. They are spiritually blind because they have rejected the Light.

Read Proverbs 26:7–12, noting the key words and phrases indicated below.

EATING VOMIT: Fools may think themselves wise, but their folly prevents them from learning that they are fools. They return to their folly as a dog returns to its vomit.

7. A PROVERB IN THE MOUTH OF FOOLS: The wisdom of man has many proverbs, which the world repeats to its own destruction: "God helps those who

help themselves," "follow your heart," "love yourself," and so forth. Yet when one is faced with genuine hardship in life, those proverbs prove as crippled as a lame man's legs.

8. ONE WHO BINDS A STONE IN A SLING: Stones are placed loosely in a sling; they are not tied in place. A sling with a stone stuck in place is a useless weapon, just as a fool is useless in a position of authority. As the stone is intended to be cast out, so also is the fool.

9. A PROVERB IN THE MOUTH OF FOOLS: Here we see this phrase again. Clearly, the writer wanted to stress that even when a fool does learn words of wisdom, he still does not know how to use them correctly. He wields them wantonly, as a drunken man might swing a scourge of thorns. The result is only injury rather than healing, both to innocent bystanders and to himself.

10. GIVES THE FOOL HIS HIRE AND THE TRANSGRESSOR HIS WAGES: The Hebrew is obscure here, resulting in many possible interpretations. The translation might be, "Much brings forth from itself all; but the reward and the wages of the fool pass away." This could mean, reasonably, that though the one who possesses much and has great ability may be able to accomplish all he wants, that is not the case when he makes use of the work of fools, who not only do not accomplish anything but also destroy everything.

11. AS A DOG RETURNS TO HIS OWN VOMIT: Dogs have the disconcerting and disgusting habit of consuming their own vomit. This vivid picture underscores the disgusting ways of the fool. His folly causes him harm, and he casts it off—only to return to it again and reconsume it. He cannot learn wisdom, because he has rejected its Source.

GOING DEEPER

Read James 3:13–17, noting the key words and phrases indicated below.

TWO WISDOMS: James warns there are two forms of wisdom: one from below and one from above. True wisdom involves loving others.

3:13. WISE AND UNDERSTANDING: *Wise* is the common Greek word for speculative knowledge and philosophy, but the Hebrews infused it with the richer meaning of skillfully applying knowledge to the matter of practical living. The word for *understanding* is used only here in the New Testament and means a specialist or professional who could skillfully apply his expertise to practical situations. James is inquiring about who is truly skilled in the art of living.

14. IF YOU HAVE BITTER ENVY: The Greek term for *bitter* was used of undrinkable water. When combined with *envy*, it defines a harsh, resentful attitude toward others. Prevailing wisdom teaches us to "keep up with the Joneses," but this only causes us to covet and envy the things that others possess. This wisdom of the world also teaches us to look after our own interests and let others take care of themselves.

AND SELF-SEEKING IN YOUR HEARTS: *Self-seeking*, sometimes translated *strife*, refers to selfish ambition that engenders antagonism and factionalism. The Greek word came to describe anyone who entered politics for selfish reasons and sought to achieve his agenda at any cost. The self-seeking person is thus one who takes advantage of every opportunity to put himself forward. This runs contrary to meekness, an essential quality of the wisdom from on high.

15. EARTHLY, SENSUAL, DEMONIC: James describes man's wisdom as: (1) limited to earth; (2) characterized by humanness, frailty, an unsanctified heart, and an unredeemed spirit; and (3) generated by Satan's forces. Earthly and sensual wisdom encourages a person to focus on temporal issues rather than see life from God's perspective.

16. CONFUSION AND EVERY EVIL THING: *Confusion* is the disorder that results from the instability and chaos of human wisdom. It leads to "every evil thing," or literally "every worthless work," which denotes things not so much intrinsically evil as simply good for nothing.

17. PEACEABLE, GENTLE, WILLING TO YIELD: Notice this list of godly qualities all center on a person's interaction with other people. The wisdom from below teaches us to look after our own interests, but the wisdom from above encourages us to put others ahead of ourselves.

UNLEASHING THE TEXT

1) According to Proverbs 1:8–14, what are some of the ways that the wicked try to entice the naïve? What is the result of following their counsel?

_____

_____

_____

2) Why is the "scoffer" unable to find wisdom (see Proverbs 14:6)? Why do those who reject Christ deny themselves from ever finding true wisdom?

_____

_____

_____

3) What types of "proverb" do fools tell themselves (see Proverbs 26:7)? What is the result of this type of wisdom in the hands of a foolish person?

_____

_____

_____

4) According to James, what are the traits of wisdom from the world? What are the traits of wisdom from God? How do we demonstrate we are wise and have understanding?

_____

_____

_____

EXPLORING THE MEANING

Wisdom from below is wise in its own eyes. Those who are "wise" in their own eyes have rejected the truth of God. They assume they can find things of lasting value in this world and give little thought to eternity. This is precisely the behavior of those who embrace the wisdom from below. Such "wisdom" is intended to keep people's focus on the things of earth, lest they stop and consider their ways, turn from their folly, and find wisdom and salvation from God.

It is this element of considering our ways that makes it so dangerous to become wise in our own eyes. If we are self-satisfied and believe we have already obtained knowledge and understanding, we will not be open to rebuke or correction. When we harden our hearts and minds against correction, we deafen our ears to the Lord's voice and become resistant to His gentle hand. We then place ourselves in the position of needing a stern rebuke and harsher discipline if we are to continue running the race.

By maintaining an eternal perspective—by seeing ourselves and the world through God's eyes rather than our own—we remain humble and open to correction. Isaiah warned, "Woe to those who call evil good, and good evil; Woe to those who are wise in their own eyes, and prudent in their own sight!" (Isaiah 5:20–21). Only when we exchange such arrogance for humility will God ensure that we finish the race well.

True wisdom only comes through the gospel. People today cite many axioms that purport to be wisdom: "follow your heart," "love yourself," and "to thine own self be true." But this so-called wisdom is absent the basis of wisdom: God's love for the world seen through the death and resurrection of Christ. When we are lost in sin, we know neither wisdom nor the author of wisdom. We believe lies about the world and think those lies are the embodiment of wisdom.

Such wisdom is not from above. Rather, true wisdom comes from having a heart transformed by God's Spirit and then having eyes that are opened to the truth in God's Word. For this reason, it is absolutely impossible for those who are separated from Christ to have any semblance of true wisdom.

As Paul wrote, "The wisdom of this world is foolishness with God . . . 'He catches the wise in their own craftiness'" (1 Corinthians 3:19). At the center of the two wisdoms stands the cross. To those who are apart from Christ, the cross represents supreme foolishness. The world assumes that if Jesus were really God, the last thing He would do is die on the cross. But for those who are saved, the cross shows the true power and wisdom of God.

We should not keep company with fools. The authors of Proverbs warn us that we tend to become like the people with whom we spend the most time. This can be beneficial for us if we spend time with those who walk in wisdom, as we will grow wiser. On the other hand, this can be detrimental to us if we choose to hang around foolish people, for "the companion of fools will be destroyed"

(Proverbs 13:20). If our close friends are fools, we will eventually begin to imitate them—and become foolish ourselves.

This does not mean we should never reach out to the lost. We were fools once as well, yet God reached out to save us. Yet while there is a place for evangelism, they should not be among our intimate circle of close friends. It is important for us to be in regular fellowship with other like-minded believers, because this will deepen our faith and provide us with role models who influence us toward godliness. As the writer of Hebrews urged, "Let us consider one another in order to stir up love and good works, not forsaking the assembling of ourselves together, as is the manner of some, but exhorting one another" (10:24–25).

Those who want to grow in wisdom will make it a point to keep company with the wise. It is proper to share the gospel with the lost, but in the process we must not become friends with the world. As James wrote, "Friendship with the world is enmity with God . . . Whoever therefore wants to be a friend of the world makes himself an enemy of God" (4:4).

REFLECTING ON THE TEXT

5) What does it mean that "the fear of the LORD is the beginning of knowledge" (Proverbs 1:7)? How does maintaining an eternal perspective allow us to reject worldly wisdom?

_____

_____

_____

6) Why are we commanded to "go from the presence of a foolish man" (Proverbs 14:7)? What is the danger of keeping company with a fool? How does a Christian balance this with reaching the lost with the gospel?

_____

_____

_____

7) What does it mean to be "self-seeking"? Give some practical examples. How is this different from true wisdom? Why does wisdom require humility before God?

_____

_____

_____

_____

8) What are some of the key differences between worldly wisdom and godly wisdom?

_____

_____

_____

_____

_____

PERSONAL RESPONSE

9) Do you tend to put others ahead of yourself? When do you find yourself doing the reverse? In what areas might the Lord be calling you to greater selflessness?

_____

_____

_____

10) Is your intimate circle of friends characterized by wisdom or folly? Whom do you find yourself imitating in daily life? How can you imitate Christ more closely?

_____

_____

_____

9

THE VIRTUOUS WOMAN

Proverbs 31:1–31

DRAWING NEAR

How does our society tend to define what makes a "successful" woman? How does it tend to define what makes a "successful" man?

THE CONTEXT

The first few chapters of Proverbs focus on a father's admonition to his son about what leading a life of true wisdom looks like and how that wisdom should shape his life. So it is only fitting the last chapter of Proverbs is a mother's advice to her son about what a godly woman should look like and what qualities she should possess. This is a woman of virtue whose worth "is far above rubies" (Proverbs 31:10).

The depiction of this woman that the mother gives to her son is presented for the benefit of both sons and daughters. To sons, it is a description of the woman they should want to marry. For daughters, it is a description of the woman they should try to emulate. While the book of Proverbs as a whole describes the life of wisdom, this last chapter in particular describes a "wife" of wisdom. It describes a married woman who appears to have some financial resources at her disposal, yet the principles outlined are widely applicable.

The woman of virtue depicted in Proverbs may seem intimidating at first. She rises before dawn and works until well after sunset. Her efforts are focused on serving others. She is capable in the domestic arts of creating clothing and gourmet meals, but she is equally competent in commerce, demonstrates shrewdness in financial affairs, and even runs a small business. Very few people possess all the qualities of the Proverbs 31 woman, but all Christians can strive to imitate her example.

The chief quality of the woman of wisdom is that she serves others with a willing heart. This is an aspect of wisdom that all God's people can acquire with the help of the Holy Spirit.

KEYS TO THE TEXT

Read Proverbs 31:1–31, noting the key words and phrases indicated below.

A MOTHER'S WARNINGS: The final chapter of Proverbs opens with "King Lemuel" remembering his mother's wise words of advice.

31:1. THE WORDS OF KING LEMUEL . . . HIS MOTHER TAUGHT HIM: The authors of Proverbs place heavy emphasis on the importance of a father's teachings, but here we see that men do not have a monopoly on wisdom—or the responsibility for teaching it to one's children. Lemuel means "belonging to God," but nothing is known of this king. Ancient Jewish tradition identified him with Solomon himself, who—perhaps because of his own sexual immorality—may have been using a pseudonym to pass on the wise teachings of his mother, Bathsheba.

2. MY SON . . . SON OF MY VOWS: The author repeated the phrase "my son" three times in this verse to indicate the serious passion of a mother's heart. Like Hannah, she had dedicated her child to the Lord (see 1 Samuel 1:11, 27–28).

3. DO NOT GIVE YOUR STRENGTH TO WOMEN: It was common for ancient kings to have many wives. We have already seen how Solomon did this very thing—and suffered greatly for it. He could attest from firsthand experience

that such behavior "destroys kings." Yet the principle applies equally to all people, young and old: sexual promiscuity is self-destructive.

5. FORGET THE LAW: Drunkenness can lead a person to disregard the teachings of God's Word, to the point of engaging in sinful behavior that one might not even consider while sober. Alcohol can pervert one's judgment and moral standards, which is all the more dangerous for anyone who holds a position of authority.

6. GIVE STRONG DRINK TO HIM WHO IS PERISHING: Such extreme situations, possibly relating to a criminal on death row or someone agonizing in pain with a terminal illness or tragic circumstance, are in utter contrast to that of the king.

8. OPEN YOUR MOUTH FOR THE SPEECHLESS: The king's duty was to uphold the case of the helpless in both physical and material crises. The monarch thus mediated the compassion of God. Christians are likewise called to defend those who cannot defend themselves. They are to plead for those who cannot plead their own case; namely, those who are otherwise ruined by their condition of weakness.

A VIRTUOUS WIFE: We are now introduced to a remarkable woman—a wife and mother who runs her household with skill.

10. WHO CAN FIND A VIRTUOUS WIFE: This next section (verses 10–31) forms an acrostic poem, with each verse beginning with the next letter of the Hebrew alphabet. The "virtuous wife" refers to a woman who is noble, morally upright, and faithful to her husband. While the scene here is of a wealthy home and the customs of the ancient Near East, the principles apply to every family. They are set forth as the prayer of every mother for her son and his future bride.

11. HER HUSBAND SAFELY TRUSTS HER: The husband does not maintain jealous guard over the virtuous wife or keep his valuables locked up so she cannot access them, as was a common ancient practice in a house of distrust. The wise woman is faithful to her marriage vows, demonstrates impeccable loyalty to her husband, and is prudent with the family's finances. Her husband's complete trust in her brings the family "no lack of gain."

13. WOOL AND FLAX . . . WILLINGLY WORKS: Wool and flax were used to make clothing and linen. The Hebrew word for *seek* means "to search for diligently." The wise woman takes extra pains to find the things her family needs,

considering both good quality and reasonable cost. She is also willing to make things for her family and not rely solely on the workmanship of others. As we have seen, the authors of Proverbs set high value on diligence and labor, often contrasting them with the indolence of the sluggard.

14. LIKE THE MERCHANT SHIPS: The woman of wisdom is like the "merchant ships" in that she goes far and wide to secure the best food for her family.

15. RISES WHILE IT IS YET NIGHT . . . PORTION FOR HER MAIDSERVANTS: The wise woman rises before dawn each day in order to have the food prepared for her family. She is selfless in serving her household, starting her day early on behalf of others, and is generous with those who help her—even with those outside her immediate family. Notice there is no hint of a grudging attitude in her selfless service toward anyone in her household.

A SUCCESSFUL BUSINESSWOMAN: The wise woman is not held hostage by the world's expectations. She finds work to do that increases her family's comfort.

16. SHE CONSIDERS A FIELD AND BUYS IT . . . SHE PLANTS A VINEYARD: Women in the ancient world were typically not involved in business transactions, yet the wise woman transcends cultural expectations in service to her family. The Hebrew word for *consider* implies careful thought and advance planning. She is not shopping for shopping's sake; rather, she has her eyes set on the future. She is not an impulse shopper, but she gives thorough consideration to her finances and searches out the most profitable purchases for her family's long-term benefit.

17. SHE GIRDS HERSELF WITH STRENGTH: The wise woman is not soft, for the work she does vigorously and with zeal has made her strong. It is a simple truism that we accomplish more when we work with effort. In this way, the wise woman is contrasted with the sluggard.

18. HER MERCHANDISE IS GOOD: The wise woman takes pride in all the labors of her hands and strives toward excellence in all she does. There is no sense here that she considers any labor too menial or that she expects the praises of others for all her hard work. She regards excellence for her family as enough reward in itself.

HER LAMP DOES NOT GO OUT BY NIGHT: This woman, who rises before daylight, also stays up well after sunset to serve her family. She keeps this before-sunrise-until-after-dark schedule because it is a priority for her to care for her household.

19. TO THE DISTAFF . . . HOLDS THE SPINDLE: These were parts of the loom, used for spinning thread and making garments. The wise woman thus takes responsibility for the clothing and appearance of her family.

20. SHE EXTENDS HER HAND TO THE POOR: The wise woman pours herself out in service to her family—and also finds time to reach out to the poor outside her household. The verbs *extends* and *reaches out* emphasize that this is a deliberate effort, not an afterthought. She can afford to be concerned for others because she has already made provision for her own. The emphasis on "her household" in these verses, however, suggests her family's needs come first.

21. SHE IS NOT AFRAID OF SNOW: The wise woman plans ahead for her family's needs and meets those needs in advance, so that when the snow falls, her husband and children are already warmly clothed. Note that she is not afraid of snow *for her household,* rather than for herself, again emphasizing her selfless motivation.

22. TAPESTRY FOR HERSELF . . . FINE LINEN AND PURPLE: This is the first time we read the wise woman has done anything for herself—and even here the tapestries she creates benefit the entire household with rich furnishings. Purple and scarlet (see verse 21) required expensive dyes and were usually worn only by royalty. The wise woman thus uses her own efforts to gather and create the very best for her family, clothing them like kings and queens.

A SUPPORTIVE WIFE: The wise woman also encourages her husband in his work and ministry, and he excels because of her support.

23. HER HUSBAND IS KNOWN IN THE GATES: To sit in the city gates indicated a position of wisdom and influence. The wise woman advances her husband's career by her vast support behind the scenes. A man's good reputation began with his home and, thus, the virtue of his wife.

24. AND SELLS THEM: With all her other responsibilities faithfully discharged, the wise woman helps support the family by making items of clothing for the purposes of trade.

25. STRENGTH AND HONOR ARE HER CLOTHING . . . IN TIME TO COME: It is striking that all other mention of clothing in these verses refers to the wise woman's family, not to herself. Her own clothing is far more valuable, as she is adorned with strength and honor, which gives her the confidence to face the future with its unexpected challenges. For the wise woman, inward beauty is more important than outward adornment. She also does not strive for immediate gain but always has her eyes focused on the future. In fact, this is one of the keys to her success, as she has placed her treasure in eternity rather than in temporal advancement.

26. OPENS HER MOUTH WITH WISDOM: As we have seen in previous studies, the authors of Proverbs address the power and importance of wise speech a great deal. The wise woman's speech is always seasoned with grace (see Colossians 4:6).

27. DOES NOT EAT THE BREAD OF IDLENESS: The wise woman is a skilled and diligent manager of the home. She does not eat the "bread of idleness" (literally, have "eyes looking everywhere"), as the sluggard does.

28. HER CHILDREN RISE UP AND CALL HER BLESSED: The wise woman has taken care to teach her children to walk in wisdom. When they grow into godly adults, they remember her example and call her blessed. There can be no higher joy for such a mother than for her children to grow up to praise her as the source of the wisdom that made them godly.

30. CHARM IS DECEITFUL AND BEAUTY IS PASSING: True holiness and virtue command permanent respect and affection, far more than charm and beauty of face and form. Contrast this with the teachings of the world today, which put such emphasis on a woman's outward appearance. Over time youthful beauty fades, but for the godly woman, time only increases the invaluable beauty of her character.

31. HER OWN WORKS PRAISE HER: While the woman of wisdom receives material reward, the praise and success she labors to bring to her family and community will be her praise. The results of all her efforts comprise her best eulogy.

GOING DEEPER

In Titus 2:1–5, we find some of Paul's teaching on the qualities of a virtuous wife in the early church. Read this passage, noting the key words and phrases indicated below.

SOUND DOCTRINE: Paul provides these instructions to his co-worker Titus to show how the believers in his church were to act. This constitutes "sound doctrine" for the church.

2:1. THINGS WHICH ARE PROPER FOR SOUND DOCTRINE: The word *sound* here means "healthy." Paul uses this word nine times in the Pastoral Epistles (five times in Titus), always in the sense that the truth produces spiritual wellbeing. The "things" Paul mentions pertain to truths, attitudes, and actions based on biblical truth. God's people must know the truth that leads to spiritual health not only to please God but also to have an effective witness to unbelievers.

2. OLDER MEN: This term refers to a man of advanced age, as opposed to an elder in the church. Paul used this word (*presbutés*) of himself in Philemon 1:9, when he was over sixty. Among the attributes listed, the older men are to be *reverent,* which is not limited just to reverence for God but also refers to being honorable and dignified to others.

3. OLDER WOMEN: This term refers to a woman who no longer had child-rearing responsibilities, typically around the age of sixty. Among the attributes Paul lists for this type of woman, she is not to be a *slanderer*—a term used thirty-four times in the New Testament to describe Satan, the arch-slanderer. Rather, she is to do "good things" that please God.

4. ADMONISH THE YOUNG WOMEN: The older wise woman, by virtue of her example of godliness, has the right and the credibility to instruct the younger women in the church. The obvious implication is that older women must exemplify the virtues they admonish.

LOVE THEIR HUSBANDS: The Greek word used for love in this verse (*phileo*) emphasizes affection. Like the other virtues mentioned here, this one is unconditional. It is based on God's will, not on a husband's worthiness.

5. TO BE DISCREET, CHASTE, HOMEMAKERS: The wise woman in the early church was to be "discreet" (meaning pure) and keep a godly home with excellence.

THAT THE WORD OF GOD MAY NOT BE BLASPHEMED: This is the purpose of godly conduct for both men and women: to eliminate any reproach on Scripture. For people to be convinced that God can save them from sin, they need to see someone who lives a holy life. When Christians claim to believe God's Word but do not obey it, they dishonor the Word. Many have mocked

God and His truth because of the sinful behavior of those who claim to be Christians.

Unleashing the Text

1) What are some of the things in Proverbs 31:1–9 that King Lemuel's mother tells her son to avoid? What are some qualities he is to embrace?

_____

_____

_____

_____

2) What are some of the ways the "virtuous wife" shows she is industrious? How does her attitude and mindset differ from that of the sluggard we studied previously?

_____

_____

_____

_____

3) How does the wise woman benefit her household? How do her husband and her children recognize her for her diligence and leadership?

_____

_____

_____

_____

4) What is the virtuous wife's true beauty? How do the characteristics she possesses apply to unmarried women? How do they apply to men?

_____

_____

_____

EXPLORING THE MEANING

The wise woman serves others rather than herself. The world urges us to serve ourselves first and foremost. The modern "self-esteem" movement teaches that we must learn to love ourselves before we can love others. However, this is a form of wisdom from below, for it is a type of false wisdom that leads us away from godliness.

The wise woman, by contrast, is always looking for ways to serve others. She puts her family first, striving to meet their immediate needs while also looking ahead to the needs of the future. When she has finished with those priorities, she turns her attention to the needs of her neighbors, reaching out generously to the poor and afflicted. In all these things, the wise woman does not see herself as a martyr but as doing for others what God has done for her.

The virtuous wife of Proverbs 31 used her resources to help others rather than satisfy her own desires. In so doing, she served the Lord cheerfully and reaped an abundant reward. As Paul reminds us, "For you, brethren, have been called to liberty; only do not use liberty as an opportunity for the flesh, but through love serve one another. For all the law is fulfilled in one word, even in this: 'You shall love your neighbor as yourself'" (Galatians 5:13–14).

The wise woman is prudent. _Prudence_ is the skill of exercising sound judgment in practical matters. The prudent person takes time to consider what course of action will be best in a given situation, rather than acting without thought. Another word for prudent is _circumspect,_ which means to see an issue or circumstance from all sides. Prudence makes a person discerning and capable of seeing the truth of a matter when others might not.

The woman of Proverbs 31 demonstrated prudence with her family's finances. She carefully considered the potential strengths and weaknesses of a field before purchasing it, examining what the investment would bring and what it would cost. She was prudent in planning ahead for the winter months, making warm clothes for others before they were needed. She was prudent in her speech, sharing gentle wisdom with others in due season, and speaking on behalf of those who could not defend themselves.

Wisdom and prudence are always seen together, as Solomon wrote in an earlier proverb: "I, wisdom, dwell with prudence, and find out knowledge and discretion" (8:12). We grow in wisdom when we take time to prayerfully consider things from God's perspective. Such wisdom is not acquired quickly, as prudence requires us to carefully deliberate before acting. This is contrary to our nature, for we often find ourselves wanting to react to circumstances immediately. But the course of wisdom consists in prudence, taking the time to ask for wisdom from God, and learning to see the world through His eyes rather than our own.

The wise woman radiates an inner beauty. Modern society places great emphasis on external appearances. We are bombarded with images of physical beauty from entertainment, while the advertising industry insists we must spend our money and time making ourselves look good according to constantly changing worldly standards. Our culture stresses physical exercise and diet, but ignores those pursuits that produce spiritual strength and character.

It is interesting that the Bible tells us nothing about Jesus' physical appearance. In fact, Isaiah suggests He was a rather plain and ordinary looking man: "He has no form or comeliness; and when we see Him, there is no beauty that we should desire Him" (Isaiah 53:2). When God became a man, the world despised Him and rejected Him. Rather than being "a god among men," who drew men to Himself with His radiant appearance, He became "a Man of sorrows and acquainted with grief. And we hid, as it were, our faces from Him; He was despised, and we did not esteem Him" (Isaiah 53:3).

God is not concerned with our physical appearance but with our spiritual character. The wise woman of Proverbs 31 understood this and focused her energies on cultivating godliness and virtue. Ironically, her inner beauty radiated outward, giving her a brilliant countenance that could not have been imitated with cosmetics. She was clothed with strength and honor and praised more than those who possessed great charm and physical beauty. God is pleased when we pursue such inner beauty. "For bodily exercise profits a little, but godliness is profitable for all things, having promise of the life that now is and of that which is to come" (1 Timothy 4:8).

REFLECTING ON THE TEXT

5) What does it mean, in practical terms, to be prudent? Give some examples of prudence from your own life or people you know.

_____

_____

_____

6) What are some of the qualities Paul listed in Titus 2:1–5 that the older men in the early church were to possess? What qualities were the older women to possess?

_____

_____

_____

7) How did the wise woman of Proverbs 31 influence her world for God? How did Paul say our conduct as Christians will influence others for God—for good or bad?

_____

_____

_____

8) In what ways does the Proverbs 31 woman go against today's culture? How do the world's teachings compare with her priorities?

_____

_____

_____

PERSONAL RESPONSE

9) Is your focus on perfecting outward appearances or on developing inner beauty? What inner qualities might the Lord be calling you to improve?

_____

_____

_____

10) Which qualities of the Proverbs 31 woman do you see in yourself? In what areas do you fall short of her high standards?

_____

_____

10

A TIME FOR EVERYTHING

Ecclesiastes 1:1–11; 3:1–22

DRAWING NEAR

What types of news stories or current events tend to make you feel the most cynical?

_____

_____

_____

THE CONTEXT

As we saw in our first study, God had given Solomon such great wisdom that he was deemed to be the wisest man of all time. The Lord had also blessed Solomon with great wealth and success over Israel's enemies. Solomon had put that wisdom to good use throughout his reign and had even recorded many of his teachings for future generations in the book of Proverbs.

But as Solomon grew older, he clearly became more cynical and despondent. His fabulous wealth, power, and prestige permitted him to participate in whatever indulgence he desired—and he had sampled all the world had to offer. Yet when he looked back, he saw that all the world's offerings had only led to emptiness, and life itself seemed nothing but vanity. Solomon had not chosen to love the Lord with his whole heart but had filled his life with compromises. What he valued in life was corrupted by his quest for meaning apart from God.

The book of Ecclesiastes encompasses Solomon's conclusions on the meaning of life. It is a profound book, but if only given a surface reading, it could seem depressing with its repeated refrain of "all is vanity" (Ecclesiastes 1:2; see also 12:8). Yet Solomon's point is that the riches of the world, the sexual pleasure found in a thousand different women, and the power invested in the king are unable to give any kind of eternal meaning to life. Thus, Ecclesiastes actually offers both a warning and an encouragement. It warns against pursuing the emptiness of the world and encourages us to trust that God is sovereign over all life's events.

There is a time for everything, Solomon writes, but we must always remember that our times are in God's hands. When we order our lives according to an understanding of His sovereignty, we gain an eternal perspective—and we avoid a life built on the vanity of vanities.

KEYS TO THE TEXT

Read Ecclesiastes 1:1–11, noting the key words and phrases indicated below.

THE VANITY OF LIFE: Solomon begins with an overview of his investigations into mankind's efforts and life work—concluding that "all is vanity."

1:2. VANITY OF VANITIES: This is Solomon's way of saying "the greatest vanity." This portrays man's view of life without redemption from sin and the promise of eternal life in Jesus Christ. It also stems from the lack of understanding of God's eternal perspective as taught in Scripture.

3. WHAT PROFIT HAS A MAN: Solomon is asking what advantage or gain we have from our own *labor*, which includes not just our livelihood but also all of our activities "under the sun." The key to understanding this seemingly pessimistic view of life is to recognize that the only lasting human efforts are those designed to accomplish God's purposes for eternity. Without an eternal perspective and purpose, all of life is futile and without purpose.

4. ONE GENERATION PASSES AWAY . . . THE EARTH ABIDES FOREVER: The essence of this comparison is the permanence of earth and the impermanence of people without "profit" or "advantage." Solomon presents life as an endless cycle of activity that, by itself, does not bring security or meaning to human experience.

9. THERE IS NOTHING NEW UNDER THE SUN: Solomon summarizes the effects of repetitious, enduring activity in God's creation over the course of many generations as compared to the brief, comparatively profitless activity of one person who fails to produce an enduring satisfaction. His conclusion is that it is wearisome. Another harsh reality comes with the realization that nothing is new and nothing will be remembered.

11. THERE IS NO REMEMBRANCE: This refers to a written record or some other object that serves as a reminder of these events, people, and things that will be short-lived.

Read Ecclesiastes 3:1–22, noting the key words and phrases indicated below.

A TIME FOR EVERY PURPOSE: God appoints "seasons" and "times" for every activity on earth. However, while earthly pursuits are good in their proper place and time, they are unprofitable when pursued as the source of joy in life.

3:1. A TIME FOR EVERY PURPOSE: Solomon lists many facets of human life in this chapter, and in most cases a person finds times and seasons that call for one or another of these endeavors. But Solomon's larger point is that God has a time and a season for all things according to His purposes, and He unfailingly turns everything to further those purposes. In this way, Solomon underscores the sovereignty of God as well as the futility of human endeavor apart from God. People may do this or that, but they can only do so in the time appointed by God.

2. TO BE BORN . . . TO DIE: Solomon groups pairs of opposites throughout this list of life's events, beginning with the most inevitable of all human experiences: birth and death. This also underscores the fact that Solomon was describing life in a fallen world, rather than the world as God originally intended it. Death entered the world through Adam's sin (see Romans 5:12), and

ever since that day, life has included frustration, struggle, and sorrows for the human race. Yet this was not what God originally intended.

TO PLANT . . . TO PLUCK WHAT IS PLANTED: Human life may include many forms of sorrow and hardship, yet the hand of God is always visible to those willing to see it. He continues to maintain the seasons and cycles that He instituted at creation, including the times of planting and harvest. God's sovereignty sustains all life on earth.

3. TO KILL . . . TO HEAL: God instituted human government after the great flood and charged Noah's descendants with the responsibility of protecting human life by putting murderers to death. "Whoever sheds man's blood, by man his blood shall be shed; for in the image of God He made man" (Genesis 9:6). The Lord's sovereign hand does bring judgment and death, but it also brings life and healing.

TO BREAK DOWN . . . TO BUILD UP: God's supreme purposes sometimes involve tearing down the works of men, and other times building up things that will last into eternity. The Lord tore down the walls of Jericho, but He established a kingdom in the line of David that will last forever through Jesus Christ.

4. TO WEEP . . . TO LAUGH . . . TO MOURN . . . TO DANCE: The normal cycle of human emotion is common to all people, as good times and hard times come on all of us. Yet the hand of God is in control of all such events, whether or not we are aware of it at the time. Weeping and laughing may be private expressions of the conditions of our lives, while mourning and dancing are more public expressions.

BUILDING AND MENDING: Solomon now turns to the issues involved in our daily labors—farming, homemaking, and even finances.

5. TO CAST AWAY STONES . . . TO GATHER STONES: Stones were "cast away" during times of peace and safety, as farmers would clear fields to make them usable for planting or grazing. Gathering stones together might imply a time of battle, or even a time of judgment, as stones could be used in warfare or in a public execution.

TO EMBRACE . . . TO REFRAIN FROM EMBRACING: The "embrace" spoken of here implies sexual intimacy. God's Word makes clear stipulations concerning the sexual embrace, and it is only appropriate within the context of marriage.

6. TO GAIN . . . TO LOSE: Here is another experience common to all people, as most of us experience times of both prosperity and of lack. Once again, God oversees all such cycles, whether or not we recognize His hand in the process.

TO KEEP . . . TO THROW AWAY: As with the cycles of economy, most people also experience times of acquiring and times of letting go of material possessions.

7. TO TEAR . . . TO SEW: People in biblical times would frequently tear their garments when they heard tragic news as an outward sign of deep grief. "Then Jacob tore his clothes, put sackcloth on his waist, and mourned for his son many days" (Genesis 37:34). The sewing of garments, however, indicates a more peaceful time of life. The Lord also speaks in Scripture of tearing and mending—as we saw in a previous study, the Lord promised that He would "tear the kingdom away" from Solomon (see 1 Kings 11:11).

TO KEEP SILENCE . . . TO SPEAK: As we have seen, Solomon wrote many proverbs concerning what times are appropriate for speech or silence (see study 5).

8. TO LOVE . . . TO HATE: It may seem incongruous that God would deem hate appropriate at certain times, yet He Himself hates sin. In the book of Revelation, the Lord speaks of hating certain false doctrines and commends those believers who share His animosity for them: "But this you have, that you hate the deeds of the Nicolaitans, which I also hate" (2:6).

9. WHAT PROFIT HAS THE WORKER: Solomon's overall point in this chapter is that man's labors have no lasting profit in themselves, for one's best efforts are worthless apart from God. This was not a dark cynicism on his part; on the contrary, a person's work can be profitable when it is done under the Lord's guiding hand. God is sovereign over all things, and those who submit to His sovereignty will discover that their labors are not in vain.

WHERE GOD FITS IN: *Solomon now turns his eyes heavenward and considers the role that God plays in man's daily affairs.*

10. THE GOD-GIVEN TASKS: Without God's involvement, all of life would be a meaningless cycle of birth and death, pleasure and pain, success

and failure. But when we see that God's hand rules purposefully over all events, we discover there is a way to live with meaning and purpose.

11. HE HAS MADE EVERYTHING BEAUTIFUL IN ITS TIME: God's self-governing hand guides all our activities and all the events of our history. He never does anything that is ugly or evil, but only that which is fitting and appropriate. Therefore, we can rest in the knowledge that God will use every event in our lives to produce His will, and He will bring beauty even out of ugliness and sorrow. The key here is the fact that He will do so in His time, not according to our schedule.

HE HAS PUT ETERNITY IN THEIR HEARTS: In the first part of this chapter, Solomon wrote about the temporal events that come into everyone's life. But God is concerned with eternity, and He uses temporal events to further His eternal plan and kingdom. He created people for His eternal purposes, and it is part of our nature to long for those things that transcend our lives on earth. This is the very reason people can become cynical and desperate when they don't have a relationship with God: they long for eternity, yet all they see are the apparently random cycles of life on earth. God has "put eternity in their hearts" so they might recognize there is more to life than that which is of this world.

NO ONE CAN FIND OUT THE WORK THAT GOD DOES: God's nature is beyond the comprehension of humans. The Bible tells us that He is sovereign over all things, that He orders the times and events of our lives, and that He uses everything—both good and evil—to further His plans. We cannot hope to understand His purposes for every situation we encounter. Instead, we must learn to trust that He is in control and that He is faithful to turn all things to His glory.

13. ENJOY THE GOOD OF ALL HIS LABOR: In accepting everything as a gift of his Creator, even in a cursed world, redeemed man is enabled to see "good" in all his work.

IT IS THE GIFT OF GOD: The key to contentment in life is to remember that all things come into our lives from the hand of God—both pleasure and pain. God's gift does not lie so much in the event itself but in the eternal good that He brings from it. Even a rich man cannot find long-term satisfaction from his wealth, because his profit is limited to this world. God brings eternal profit to all His children, and He does so through our failures as well as our successes.

14. FEAR BEFORE HIM. Acknowledging God's enduring and perfect work becomes grounds for reverence, worship, and meaning. Apart from God, man's works are inadequate.

ALL IS VANITY: Solomon concludes with the realization that all life ends in death, regardless of how one lives. Thus, the only thing that matters is the judgment of God.

16. WICKEDNESS WAS THERE: When we view life from a human standpoint, we are likely to fall into hopeless pessimism because we see the injustice and wickedness in the world around us. However, Christians must remember that God is always in control, even when we see wickedness in the place of judgment and iniquity in the place of righteousness. Man sees only what is temporal, but God sees all things from an eternal point of view.

17. GOD SHALL JUDGE . . . FOR THERE IS A TIME: The culminating issue of Solomon's "appointed time" discussion is that there is a time for judgment. The unsaved do not acknowledge the fact that God will one day judge the living and the dead. The world teaches that there are no eternal consequences to our actions, but God reminds His people that He will one day judge all men. This knowledge can also bring comfort to God's people, as we sometimes are called on to endure the world's corruption of truth and justice.

19. MAN HAS NO ADVANTAGE OVER ANIMALS: The ultimate fate of both man and beast is to die. Solomon isn't looking at final, eternal destinies, but at what all earthly flesh shares in common alive. If people try to find meaning in life apart from God, their lives will be as futile as an animal's, because death awaits them both. However, unlike the animals, humans will live forever. So in that sense, a person who lives his life apart from God is actually *worse* off than an animal, because at least animals escape judgment.

ALL IS VANITY: This is the ultimate conclusion that unsaved people are forced to reach. If there were no God in control of men's eternal destiny, all of life would be futile and vain.

20. FROM THE DUST . . . TO DUST: Here Solomon alludes to God's words in Genesis 3:19 in the broadest sense: "In the sweat of your face you shall eat bread till you return to the ground, for out of it you were taken; for dust you are, and to dust you shall return." *All* of living creation will die and go to the grave—neither heaven nor hell is considered here.

21. THE SPIRIT OF THE SONS OF MEN: A person's breath or physical life appears on the surface to be little different than that of an animal. However, in reality our soul dramatically differs in that God has made us eternal.

UNLEASHING THE TEXT

1) What are Solomon's conclusions about life in Ecclesiastes 1:1–11? What is his main point about the work we do on this earth outside of God's plans and purposes?

_____

_____

_____

_____

2) What does Solomon reveal about the nature of life in Ecclesiastes 3:1–8?

_____

_____

_____

_____

3) Why does Solomon say there is "a time to hate" (Ecclesiastes 3:8)? What might be some examples of godly hatred?

_____

_____

_____

4) What does Solomon mean when he writes that God "has made everything beautiful in its time" (verse 11)? When have you seen God make something beautiful out of an unpleasant situation in your life?

_____

_____

_____

EXPLORING THE MEANING

God is sovereign, and He uses every event of our lives for His purposes. God originally created the world without sin or death, but when Adam and Eve disobeyed God's command (see Genesis 2–3), their sin brought the curse of death and sorrow on the entire world. As a result, today we live in a fallen world. Our lives are marked by times of suffering and grief, and ultimately each of us will face physical death.

God was not caught by surprise when Adam sinned. In fact, He designed the world in such a way as to receive glory as the Savior of humankind from our sin. Jesus was "the Lamb slain from the foundation of the world" (Revelation 13:8), and through His sacrifice on the cross we can be reconciled to God. If we accept Jesus' sacrifice and choose to have a relationship with God, everything in our life becomes meaningful. There is nothing in life that falls outside the realm of God's control, and He uses all things to further His own timeless plan.

God's plan for us includes making us more like His Son, Jesus, and He uses every event to advance this cause—including events that may bring heartache for a time. It can be easy to forget this fact when we are faced with difficulty, yet we will find such times easier to endure if we rest in God's sovereignty. As Paul reminds us, "All things work together for good to those who love God, to those who are the called according to His purpose" (Romans 8:28).

The world's philosophies lead to cynicism and despair. Secular science teaches that humans evolved from random cells and there is no God who oversees and sustains the world. This teaching forces people to conclude that life's events are random. After all, if there is no God in control, then everything that happens is mere chance. If there is no judgment, then this life is all that matters. And if everyone dies, then this life does not matter that much anyway.

The false religions of the world teach that humans can somehow overcome this empty cycle of life and death through their own efforts—by trusting in good works to escape judgment or by reincarnating again and again until they attain a sinless state. Such views lead only to despair, because no one can live a sinless life, and no one can ever hope to defeat death. People who strive to overcome the curse of death by their own labors will ultimately become hopeless and cynical because they will discover they are powerless to do so—yet they will not know the God who has already defeated death.

However, as believers in Christ, we should never become cynical because we know that life is more than a terrestrial cycle of ups and downs. There is a God who created all things, and He is in absolute control of every event that happens of our lives. Nothing can separate us from the love of God, and this assurance will keep us from despair.

We must keep our focus on eternity, not the things of the world. As we have seen in previous studies, Solomon began his reign with great wisdom and great focus on the eternal perspectives of God. But over time he lost sight of that focus and began to concern himself more with the temporal things of this world. As a result, he turned away from full obedience to God and followed after the empty practices of paganism.

Christians today can also lose their eternal focus, and the results for us are just as disastrous as they were for Solomon so many years ago. If we allow the world's values to creep into our thinking, we run the risk of losing sight of God's divine perspective—and this, as we have seen, leads only to despair. We can keep our focus on eternity by remembering that we will live forever with God and that this temporal life is just that: *temporary*.

Our times of prosperity can be just as misleading for us as times of suffering, for wealth and success can make us forget that the things of this world will pass away. John reflected this understanding when he wrote, "Do not love the world or the things in the world. If anyone loves the world, the love of the Father is not in him. For all that is in the world—the lust of the flesh, the lust of the eyes, and the pride of life—is not of the Father" (1 John 2:15–16).

REFLECTING ON THE TEXT

5) Why does Solomon say that there is "a time for every purpose" (Ecclesiastes 3:1)? What does this mean from God's eternal perspective?

_____

_____

_____

6) What is each person's God-given task? What is your God-given task at present? How are you actively going about fulfilling that task?

_____

_____

_____

7) What season of life are you in right now? How might God be using your circumstances to further His plan for your life?

_____

_____

_____

8) List some of the ways that you have seen God's sovereignty in your life. How can these events encourage you to trust Him more in the future?

_____

_____

_____

PERSONAL RESPONSE

9) Where is your focus in life: on eternity or on the world? What priorities might the Lord want you to change?

_____

_____

_____

10) How do you respond to disappointment or hardship? Is your tendency toward cynicism or despair, or do you trust God to work things to His glory? Explain.

_____

_____

_____

11

THE FULL DUTY OF MAN

Ecclesiastes 2:12–26; 9:1–5; 12:1–14

DRAWING NEAR

How do you judge the contributions you have made in this world? What legacy do you hope to leave behind for your children and grandchildren?

_____

_____

_____

THE CONTEXT

There are several conclusions we can reach when we look back on the life of Solomon. Clearly, God had blessed the beginning of his reign by giving him great wisdom, wealth, and prestige in the world. Solomon had used that wisdom, at first, to rule God's people justly, so that "all Israel . . . saw that the wisdom of God was in him to administer justice" (1 Kings 3:28). Solomon later fulfilled the task his father, David, left for him in constructing the temple. This structure, and the palace he built, were considered wonders of the known world.

God also blessed Solomon's reign by giving him great power and victory over his enemies. In fact, the Israelite army was the best equipped and most powerful fighting force on earth during the time of his reign. "Solomon reigned over all kingdoms from the River to the land of the Philistines, as far as the border of Egypt" (4:21). He was the first leader to solidify control of the trade routes connecting Africa, Europe, and Asia, which enabled him to sample all the world had to offer. There was no pursuit or pleasure that he denied himself.

Yet near the end of his life, Solomon solemnly declared that all his pursuits in life were empty and meaningless. "Therefore I hated life because the work that was done under the sun was distressing to me, for all is vanity and grasping for the wind" (Ecclesiastes 2:17). In his later years, Solomon came to acknowledge that death comes to everyone—the fool and the wise one alike—regardless of how they lived. It is a refrain that Solomon often repeats in Ecclesiastes—his final assessment of all his life's accomplishments and indulgences.

However, there is a much deeper and more important theme running through Ecclesiastes, and it is a message of hope, not of despair. There *is* a way for a man or woman to live a fulfilling life: by living for the glory of God! The key to doing this, as Solomon states at the end of the book, is to "fear God and keep His commandments" (12:13). When Christians live with this injunction in mind, they will avoid the pessimistic despair of a life of vanity.

KEYS TO THE TEXT

Read Ecclesiastes 2:12–26, noting the key words and phrases indicated below.

> *HATING LIFE: Solomon opens this passage with a note of cynicism and hopelessness. What is the point of life's toil, he asks, if it all ends in death?*

2:14. THE FOOL WALKS IN DARKNESS: The fool is not a person who is mentally deficient but morally bankrupt. It is not that the fool *cannot* learn wisdom, but that he *will not*. The fool refuses to know, fear, and obey God, and so he walks in darkness.

15. IT ALSO HAPPENS TO ME: Human wisdom suffers another crucial shortcoming in that it leaves both the wise and the fool empty-handed at the threshold of death.

17. I HATED LIFE: As previously noted, Solomon had tasted all that life had to offer: pleasure, work, pursuits of the flesh, and even human wisdom. Yet he had found them all empty and declared all were mere vanity. He discovered

the world cannot offer anything of lasting worth because everything on earth ends with death—and the same death comes on the wise man and the fool.

UNDER THE SUN: The concept of "under the sun" is the important element in Solomon's pursuit of meaning. It indicates he had been searching for a source of sustaining value in temporal areas and had found none. Under the sun, he had examined all that is available in this earthly life, but it had all proved to be vain. Trying to find lasting significance apart from God is like "grasping for the wind" (1:14).

18. THE MAN WHO WILL COME AFTER ME: It is futile to amass great wealth and power, for even those who build great empires or extensive business monopolies will one day die, and their vast wealth and power will fall into the hands of someone else.

19. HE WILL RULE OVER ALL MY LABOR: The man who strives his whole life to acquire great wealth is merely doing all the hard work for someone else's benefit. The one who inherits that wealth may prove to be a fool and use his riches in ways his predecessor never intended. This would prove to be literally true in Solomon's case because his son, Rehoboam, was a colossal fool who ruined the powerful empire he inherited (see 1 Kings 12).

20. THE LABOR IN WHICH I HAD TOILED UNDER THE SUN: Solomon underscored that all these pursuits were for things found *under* the sun. It is a vain pursuit to chase after prosperity and power, for they are of this world and will remain *under the sun* even after the one who acquired them has departed into eternity.

FINDING SATISFACTION IN LABOR: One way that we can find some solace in life is to delight ourselves in the work God gives us to do.

23. HIS WORK BURDENSOME: Pursuit of worldly gain, of things found under the sun, is burdensome because we are always at risk of losing it all. This burden weighs heavily on our minds to the point of making our weary souls lose sleep with worry. The more we have, the more we end up worrying about losing it.

24. HIS SOUL SHOULD ENJOY GOOD IN HIS LABOR: Solomon acknowledged that even life's material blessings are from the hand of God, for He created all things to be good (see Genesis 1:31). It is not wrong to enjoy the blessings of life, especially when we take delight in the work God provides, but

the problem comes when we thinks this enjoyment somehow gives meaning to our lives. The fact is, the work is meaningless in and of itself, but it can be a tool our Creator uses to deepen our relationship with Him.

26. A MAN WHO IS GOOD IN HIS SIGHT: Solomon returns to the realization that God's perspective is the only truth in this world. The world might declare a person to be good and wise if he or she acquires great wealth or produces impressive works, but that is not God's view. Someone who is good in God's sight is a person "after His own heart"—one who builds his or her life on the Word of God (see Acts 13:22).

Read Ecclesiastes 9:1–5, noting the key words and phrases indicated below.

BUT DEATH STILL COMES: Even when we find satisfaction in work, death will still end it all. Every living thing in this world will ultimately end the same way.

9:1. THEIR WORKS ARE IN THE HAND OF GOD: Viewed from a temporal perspective, the same result comes to all people—both righteous and unrighteous—in that everyone experiences physical death. But God sees all things from an eternal perspective, and the eternal outcome of a person's life may be very different from his or her outcome on this fallen planet. Everything is in the hand of God, and He is sovereign over the affairs of all humans.

PEOPLE KNOW NEITHER LOVE NOR HATRED: That is, we can only see what is present and past, but not what awaits us in the future. No matter what successes or failures we experience in his life, we cannot predict what God will do tomorrow. We are given work to do, but God controls the results.

2. ONE EVENT HAPPENS TO THE RIGHTEOUS AND THE WICKED: Solomon again reiterates that death comes to all equally, regardless of how they lived their lives. Furthermore, death ends the labors and deeds of each person, and no one can carry any secular accomplishments into eternity. The truly wise person will lay up sacred treasure in heaven—a treasure that will last forever (see Matthew 6:19–20).

4. A LIVING DOG IS BETTER THAN A DEAD LION: This proverb reflects the characteristic wisdom of man, pointing out that even the lowliest creature is better off alive than the most noble creature is dead. There is truth in this on

a temporal level, but it suggests that death is the end of human existence—and that is not the case. In the eternal perspective, the righteous are better off than the wicked, whether dead or alive.

5. THE DEAD KNOW NOTHING, AND THEY HAVE NO MORE REWARD: This again reflects human wisdom—that a person's labors end with the grave. Conversely, God's wisdom teaches that our labors on earth can bring us eternal rewards. The wise, therefore, will use their time on earth to lay up eternal treasure, for after death no one has any further opportunity for eternal gain or loss. Our decision is made when we die, and we can never return to life to change our mind. Therefore, we must labor for the Lord while we have the opportunity (see John 9:4).

Read Ecclesiastes 12:1–14, noting the key words and phrases indicated below.

TRIALS OF OLD AGE: Solomon paints a gloomy picture of old age to remind young people that they will not enjoy the blessing of a godly old age if they do not remember their Creator while young.

12:1. REMEMBER NOW YOUR CREATOR: Solomon urges his young listeners to remember they are God's property and should serve Him from the start of their years, not at the end of their lives when their service is limited by their remaining days on earth. In this way they can be godly and finish out their final years with blessings: "The silver-haired head is a crown of glory, if it is found in the way of righteousness" (Proverbs 16:31).

2. SUN AND THE LIGHT . . . ARE NOT DARKENED: Youth is typically depicted as the time of dawning light, and old age as the time of twilight's gloom.

3. KEEPERS OF THE HOUSE TREMBLE: In this verse Solomon describes the effects of old age. The "keepers of the house" refers to the hands and arms that protect the body, as guards do a palace, which shake in old age. The "strong men" refers to the legs, which, like supporting pillars, weaken over time. The "grinders," or teeth, fall out. The eyes, which "look through the windows," grow dim.

4. THE DOORS ARE SHUT: The "doors" that are shut refers to lips that do not have much to say. The "sound of grinding" refers to little eating, when the sound of masticating is low. "Rises up" refers to light sleep, and "daughters of music" refers to the ear and voice that once loved the sound of music.

5. AFRAID OF HEIGHT, AND OF TERRORS: This refers to the fear of falling and other terrors experienced in old age. The "almond tree blossoms" speaks of graying hair (white blossoms among dark trees). The reference to the "mourners" indicates the funeral is near.

6. SILVER CORD IS LOOSED . . . GOLDEN BOWL IS BROKEN: All the actions Solomon incorporates in this verse—"loosed," "broken," "shattered," "broken"—portray death as tragic and irreversible. The "silver cord" could refer to a lamp hanging from a silver chain that breaks with age, smashing the lamp, though some suggest it refers to the spinal cord. The "golden bowl" that breaks possibly refers to the brain.

PITCHER SHATTERED . . . WHEEL BROKEN: Wells required a wheel with a rope attached in order to lower the pitcher for water. This perhaps pictures the fountain of blood, the heart.

7. THE DUST WILL RETURN . . . THE SPIRIT WILL RETURN: Solomon recalls Genesis 2:7 and 3:19 as he contemplates the end of the aging process. The sage ends his message with the culmination of a human life: "The LORD gave, and the LORD has taken away" (Job 1:21).

FEAR AND OBEY: *Solomon gives hope to his readers in his summarization of his answer to life's questions: fear God and obey His Word.*

11. LIKE GOADS . . . LIKE WELL-DRIVEN NAILS: Solomon had two shepherd's tools in view here. The *goad* was used to motivate reluctant animals, while *well-driven nails* were used to secure those animals that might otherwise wander into dangerous territory. Both goads and nails picture aspects of applied wisdom "given by one Shepherd." True wisdom has its source in God alone.

12. OF MAKING MANY BOOKS THERE IS NO END: Books written on any subject other than God's revealed wisdom will only proliferate the uselessness of man's thinking.

13. THE CONCLUSION OF THE WHOLE MATTER: As we have seen, Solomon had explored everything the world had to offer and had found it all to be vanity. At the end of his quest, he returned to the true wisdom of his youth, recognizing that lasting value and meaning can only be found in a relationship with God.

Fear God and keep His commandments: This summarizes the entire purpose of life from an eternal point of view. To "fear" God is to hold Him in reverence and honor Him as Lord of all creation. Keeping His commandments does not necessarily preclude a person from enjoying work or finding delight in the life that God grants. In fact, the contrary is the case: the person who fears God and keeps His commandments will find true satisfaction and peace in life, because he or she knows that God is in control of all things.

14. God will bring every work into judgment: The wise man always remembers that a time is coming when God will bring unbelievers into eternal judgment (see Revelation 20:11–15). Christians will never face eternal judgment, yet we will face God's assessment of our lives, when He will test our works to see whether they were done for His glory. That which we do for His glory will be like gold, silver, and precious stones, while that which we do for earthly gain will be burned up like wood, hay, and straw (see 1 Corinthians 3:10–15).

Unleashing the Text

1) Why did Solomon frequently repeat the phrase "under the sun" in Ecclesiastes 2:17–22? To what was he referring? What did this reveal about his priorities?

_____

_____

_____

2) What caused Solomon to find no value in his labors? How can a person find joy in work?

_____

_____

_____

3) What is Solomon's purpose in painting such a bleak outlook on old age in Ecclesiastes 12:1–8? What is his message for the young?

_____

_____

_____

4) Why did Solomon declare that everything in life is vanity?

_____

_____

_____

Exploring the Meaning

Life is meaningless apart from God. The world would have us believe that fabulous wealth, far-reaching power, and the wisdom to use it well are the ultimate goals of our time on earth. Yet Solomon possessed each of these things in abundance and found them all to be pointless—the "vanity of vanities" (Ecclesiastes 12:8). Toward the end of his life, as he reflected on all the indulgences he had enjoyed, he saw no meaning in them whatsoever.

Solomon's problem, as we saw in previous studies, was that he had departed from an obedient walk with God. "His wives turned his heart after other gods; and his heart was not loyal to the Lord his God" (1 Kings 11:4). Solomon had abandoned the Source of wisdom and had begun to seek fulfillment in the things the world has to offer. Yet for all his searching, he found nothing that could bring lasting satisfaction. All was vanity because the things he tried were devoid of God's blessing.

God wants His children to live fruitful and satisfying lives, though that also includes times of discipline and suffering. Satisfaction comes not from enjoying good things on earth but from walking in a relationship with the Author of all that is good. Joy and meaning are found only in the Giver of good gifts, not in the gifts themselves. When we walk in obedience to God's Word, we find contentment with the lives that God gives us. Apart from such obedience, even the best things of the world are empty and vain.

Store up treasure in heaven, not on earth. As a young man, Solomon had been presented with an intriguing proposition from the Lord: "Ask! What shall I give you?" (1 Kings 3:5). The young king had made the right choice in asking for God's wisdom, so that he might rule over the Israelites well and be pleasing to the Lord. God blessed Solomon not only with wisdom but also with riches and power. Later, Jesus would refer to "Solomon in all his glory" (Matthew 6:29).

At this point Solomon had his eyes focused on eternity and was eager to lay up treasures in the kingdom of God. However, as we have seen, he gradually took his eyes off eternity and focused them on the things of earth—and the book of Ecclesiastes tells us the result of that focus: "vanity of vanities." The trinkets and baubles of this world can seem very appealing to our fleshly eyes, but no worldly possession or accomplishment lasts forever. All temporal things are just that: temporal and temporary.

Human nature is such that we keep our eyes focused on the things we value most, like a king watching over his vast treasure hoard. Wherever we place our treasure is exactly where we will fix our attention. But our true treasure lies in eternity, where we can never lose the things God gives us. This is why Jesus said, "Do not lay up for yourselves treasures on earth, where moth and rust destroy and where thieves break in and steal; but lay up for yourselves treasures in heaven, where neither moth nor rust destroys and where thieves do not break in and steal. For where your treasure is, there your heart will be also" (Matthew 6:19–21).

The day of judgment is coming. People who lay up treasure in this world alone do so in part because they have lost sight of eternity. The world teaches us this life is all that matters and, more specifically, there is no God to whom we will give an account. And if there is no God, and this life is all we get, we might as well live as we choose! This is at the root of the modern cult of self-love and self-esteem, as people today make pleasing themselves their sole aim.

But the Bible makes it clear that God will one day judge the earth and every person who has ever lived will stand before Him. Those who have rejected Christ as their Savior will face the dreadful judgment seat of Christ, when the Lord will open the Book of Life and not find their names written in it (see Revelation 20:11–15). They will be cast out of His presence for all eternity. Christians will not face this terrible day of judgment, because our names are already permanently written in God's Book of Life. Yet the Lord will still examine our lives, giving and withholding rewards according to our level of obedience to His Word.

It is important for us to keep these things in mind as we go through our lives, remembering always that God will one day hold us accountable for how we live. As Paul reminds us, "Each one's work will become clear; for the Day will declare it, because it will be revealed by fire; and the fire will test each one's work, of what sort it is. If anyone's work which he has built on it endures, he will receive a reward. If anyone's work is burned, he will suffer loss; but he himself will be saved, yet so as through fire" (1 Corinthians 3:13–15).

REFLECTING ON THE TEXT

5) What did Solomon mean when he said that "the righteous and the wise and their works are in the hand of God" (Ecclesiastes 9:1)? What are the implications of this truth?

_____

_____

_____

_____

6) What does it mean to "fear God and keep His commandments" (Ecclesiastes 12:13)? How is this done?

_____

_____

_____

_____

7) What part did the day of judgment play in Solomon's thinking? What part does it play in your own priorities?

8) Have you ever gone through a time when you hated life? What caused your despair? What brought you out of it?

PERSONAL RESPONSE

9) Where is your treasure? Is your focus on eternity, or is it on the here and now?

10) Are you prepared for the day of judgment? Is your name written in God's Book of Life? If not, what is preventing you from asking God to write it there right now?

12

REVIEWING KEY PRINCIPLES

DRAWING NEAR

As you look back at each of the studies in 1 Kings 1–11, Proverbs, and Ecclesiastes, what is the one thing that stood out to you the most? What is one new perspective you have learned?

_____

_____

_____

THE CONTEXT

During the course of these eleven studies, you have examined the life of Solomon, the wisest man who ever lived. In the process you have gained a deeper understanding of God's great gift of wisdom, which comes only through believing in his Son, Jesus Christ. You have also gotten to know a number of interesting "characters," including those who exhibited wisdom and those who lived in folly. But one theme has remained constant throughout these studies: *God is faithful,* and those who obey Him will grow faithfulness as well.

One who is wise must first and foremost have a deep reverence for the character and commands of God, for this is the foundation of all true wisdom.

Such a person is open to correction and will work constantly to know God and obey His Word. But the world also offers a counterfeit form of wisdom, and Christians must always be on guard to avoid being misled by this "wisdom from below."

The following are a few of the major principles we have found during our study. There are many more we don't have room to reiterate, so take some time to review the earlier studies—or, better still, to meditate on the Scripture that we have covered. As you do, ask the Holy Spirit to give you wisdom and insight into His Word. He will not refuse.

EXPLORING THE MEANING

Wisdom is moral, not merely intellectual. When the Bible speaks of wisdom, it is not talking about a person's intelligence. From God's perspective, wisdom is a moral quality. A wise person lives life skillfully because he has discernment and can distinguish between good and evil. A person can be a mathematical genius or a scholar and still be considered a fool if he does not understand the truths of Scripture. A person can be a smart fool but not a wise atheist.

Wisdom has nothing to do with a person's inherent natural gifts. It is not gained through a good education, nor is it made more available to certain social classes or income brackets. Wisdom comes only from God, and it is a gift He gives to those who ask for it. Solomon described wisdom and understanding as "more precious than rubies" (Proverbs 3:15). Nothing we desire can ever compare with wisdom, "for her proceeds are better than the profits of silver" (verse 14). Wisdom can bring long life, riches, and great honor, and it enables a person to live a peaceable and pleasant life (see verses 16–17).

The Word of God contains the words of life, and they are a treasure beyond anything the world has to offer. As David wrote, "The law of the LORD is perfect . . . more to be desired . . . than much fine gold; sweeter also than honey and the honeycomb. Moreover by them Your servant is warned, and in keeping them there is great reward" (Psalm 19:7, 10–11).

The Lord does not tolerate syncretism. Syncretism is the act of combining elements of diverse religious philosophies into a new form of worship. Solomon attempted to do this when he added pagan practice to the prescribed worship of God, drawing in elements from the worship of a variety of false gods. The Lord had expressly forbidden His people from intermarrying for this very reason, and Solomon's paganism led to the loss of his kingdom.

The modern church has frequently fallen into syncretism as well, incorporating worldly principles and ideas into the Word of God. This can be seen in the addition of New Age ideas, evolutionary thinking, self-help approaches to sinful behaviors, or pandering to cultural trends. Christians act in an unwise manner when they attempt to add to the written Word of God, because it is complete already and as pertinent today as when it was first written.

As we have seen during the course of these studies, the world offers a form of wisdom that can appear sound at first glance, but its source is not from God. This "wisdom" is from below, not from above. Christians must be constantly on guard to prevent such false wisdom from being added to the sound teachings of Scripture.

Life presents a choice: wisdom or folly. Life in this fallen world offers countless options that lead away from God and toward destruction, but in reality there are only two paths: the path of wisdom or the path of folly. While the world has all manner of counsel and advice, everything it offers is, in fact, on the same path. It all leads to destruction.

So-called "wisdom" that is from the world is easier to obtain and easier to follow than wisdom that comes from God. For this reason, the path of the world is wide, and it seems as if everyone is on it. But the path of true wisdom is narrow, and there are few who find it. Consider how Jesus described it: "Wide is the gate and broad is the way that leads to destruction, and there are many who go in by it" (Matthew 7:13). This is contrasted with the path of wisdom: "Narrow is the gate and difficult is the way which leads to life, and there are few who find it" (verse 14).

Fortunately, we are not alone! God gives His Spirit to Christians to indwell us, teach us the wisdom from above, and enable us to live with skill and become more like Christ. He is the Counselor, the one who shows us all things that are true and who enables us to follow the path of wisdom.

Our words affect our actions and the actions of others. Life seems to be filled with talk. The media bombards us with words, politicians prate ceaselessly about the economy and social affairs, and people debate their opinions about everything under the sun. "It's all just words," we say, implying that words without action have no meaning.

But the Bible teaches us that our words have a powerful effect, both on ourselves and on others. James used the illustration of a wildfire to indicate the destruction that can be caused by idle or careless speech. It can burn the person who utters it and scald the person who hears it. It can also spread its destruction in a wide circle as one person's words are repeated by another. Each speaker's utterances lead to actions by himself or those around him.

However, this principle can also work in a positive way. As we learn to speak words of wisdom, we increase the likelihood that we will act in wisdom and encourage others to live in godliness. Consider James's analogy of a ship under the power of the wind: the pilot guides the rudder, and the rudder steers the ship. When we submit to the guidance of the Holy Spirit, He guides us in the use of our tongues, and our tongues can steer us into Christlike character.

Laziness leads to personal destruction. The sluggard has an excessive love for rest and relaxation. Again, these things in themselves are not sinful—the sin comes when leisure pursuits become a consuming passion. The person who sleeps or plays when he should be working will be overtaken by poverty, and it will come on him unexpectedly and irresistibly like an armed robber. The individual with too much time on his hands will also find things to do with that time that will cause harm to himself and to others, such as becoming a busybody who meddles in affairs that are none of his business.

This principle, of course, is not limited to laziness; it holds true for any fleshly passion we allow to rule our lives. The sin of laziness is just one of many ways that Christians can permit their flesh to govern their lives, and the result is always crippling. As Paul confessed, "I know that in me (that is, in my flesh) nothing good dwells; for to will is present with me, but how to perform what is good I do not find . . . O wretched man that I am! Who will deliver me from this body of death?" (Romans 7:18, 24).

The answer to this question is Jesus Christ—it is He who delivers us from the body of sin and from the eternal destruction that would otherwise be our fate. Thanks to Him, we have the power and presence of the Holy Spirit working in our lives, and He gives us the ability to subdue the flesh and obey His Word. And we *need* that. The ways of the flesh lead to destruction, but the ways of God lead to wisdom and eternal life.

We do not run the race alone or under our own power. The world of athletic competition features some amazing accomplishments. Runners set world records for speed, mountain climbers demonstrate incredible endurance, skydivers defy death by leaping from great heights—there are countless feats of prowess being undertaken by daring men and women all over the world every day. But there is one thing that all these feats have in common: they are within the realm of possibility for human endeavor.

That is not the case when it comes to the Christian race. We are called to be like Christ, but there is no person on earth who can accomplish that feat in his or her own power. We are all born under the curse of sin, and none of us can overcome that curse. Left to our own devices, we could never hope to live as Christ lived, for He was without sin. Thank God we are not left to our own devices! God has given His Spirit to each believer—the very same Spirit that raised Christ from the dead (see Romans 8:1). It is through the power and guidance of the Holy Spirit that we overcome the sinful nature that holds us captive.

Paul once cried, "Oh, what a miserable person I am! Who will free me from this life that is dominated by death?" But no sooner had he uttered this lament than the answer came to him: "Thank God! The answer is in Jesus Christ our Lord" (Romans 7:24–25 NLT). We are called on to endure, to persevere in the race to the end, that we might attain the prize that never fades away—but we are also empowered *by* God Himself to accomplish this task. As long as we remain open to His correction, He will enable us to finish strong.

True wisdom only comes through the gospel. People today cite many axioms that purport to be wisdom: "follow your heart," "love yourself," and "to thine own self be true." But this so-called wisdom is absent the basis of wisdom: God's love for the world seen through the death and resurrection of Christ. When we are lost in sin, we know neither wisdom nor the author of wisdom. We believe lies about the world and think those lies are the embodiment of wisdom.

Such wisdom is not from above. Rather, true wisdom comes from having a heart transformed by God's Spirit and then having eyes that are opened to the truth in God's Word. For this reason, it is absolutely impossible for those who are separated from Christ to have any semblance of true wisdom.

As Paul wrote, "The wisdom of this world is foolishness with God . . . 'He catches the wise in their own craftiness'" (1 Corinthians 3:19). At the center of the two wisdoms stands the cross. To those who are apart from Christ, the cross represents supreme foolishness. The world assumes that if Jesus were really God, the last thing He would do is die on the cross. But for those who are saved, the cross shows the true power and wisdom of God.

We must keep our focus on eternity, not the things of the world. As we have seen in previous studies, Solomon began his reign with great wisdom and great focus on the eternal perspectives of God. But over time he lost sight of that focus and began to concern himself more with the temporal things of this world. As a result, he turned away from full obedience to God and followed after the empty practices of paganism.

Christians today can also lose their eternal focus, and the results for us are just as disastrous as they were for Solomon so many years ago. If we allow the world's values to creep into our thinking, we run the risk of losing sight of God's divine perspective—and this, as we have seen, leads only to despair. We can keep our focus on eternity by remembering that we will live forever with God and that this temporal life is just that: *temporary.*

Our times of prosperity can be just as misleading for us as times of suffering, for wealth and success can make us forget that the things of this world will pass away. John reflected this understanding when he wrote, "Do not love the world or the things in the world. If anyone loves the world, the love of the Father is not in him. For all that is in the world—the lust of the flesh, the lust of the eyes, and the pride of life—is not of the Father" (1 John 2:15–16).

Store up treasure in heaven, not on earth. As a young man, Solomon had been presented with an intriguing proposition from the Lord: "Ask! What shall I give you?" (1 Kings 3:5). The young king had made the right choice in asking for God's wisdom, so that he might rule over the Israelites well and be pleasing to the Lord. God blessed Solomon not only with wisdom but also with riches and power. Later, Jesus would refer to "Solomon in all his glory" (Matthew 6:29).

At this point Solomon had his eyes focused on eternity and was eager to lay up treasures in the kingdom of God. However, as we have seen, he gradually took his eyes off eternity and focused them on the things of earth—and the book of Ecclesiastes tells us the result of that focus: "vanity of vanities." The trinkets and baubles of this world can seem very appealing to our fleshly eyes. But no worldly possession or accomplishment lasts forever. All temporal things are just that: temporal and temporary.

Human nature is such that we keep our eyes focused on the things we value most, like a king watching over his vast treasure hoard. Wherever we place our treasure is exactly where we will fix our attention. But our true treasure lies in eternity, where we can never lose the things God gives us. This is why Jesus said, "Do not lay up for yourselves treasures on earth, where moth and rust destroy and where thieves break in and steal; but lay up for yourselves treasures in heaven, where neither moth nor rust destroys and where thieves do not break in and steal. For where your treasure is, there your heart will be also" (Matthew 6:19–21).

Unleashing the Text

1) Which of the concepts or principles in this study have you found to be the most encouraging? Why?

_____

_____

_____

_____

2) Which of the concepts or principles have you found most challenging? Why?

_____

_____

_____

_____

3) What aspects of "walking with God" are you already doing in your life? Which areas need strengthening?

_____

_____

_____

4) To which of the characters that we've studied have you most been able to relate? How might you emulate that person in your own life?

_____

_____

_____

PERSONAL RESPONSE

5) Have you taken a definite stand for Jesus Christ? Have you accepted His free gift of salvation? If not, what is preventing you from doing so?

_____

_____

_____

6) What areas of your life have been most convicted during this study? What exact things will you do to address these convictions? Be specific.

_____

_____

_____

7) What have you learned about the character of God during this study? How has this insight affected your worship or prayer life?

_____

_____

_____

8) What are some specific things you want to see God do in your life in the coming month? What are some things you intend to change in your own life during that time? (Return to this list in one month and hold yourself accountable to fulfill these things.)

_____

_____

_____

If you would like to continue in your study of the Old Testament, read the next title in this series: *1 Kings 12–22: The Kingdom Divides.*

ALSO AVAILABLE

In this study, John MacArthur guides readers through an in-depth look at the Israelites' conquest of the Promised Land, beginning with the miraculous parting of the Jordan River, continuing through the victories and setbacks as the people settled into Canaan, and concluding with the time of the judges. Studies include close-up examinations of Rahab, Ruth, and Samson, as well as careful considerations of doctrinal themes such as "The Sin of Achan" and the role of "The Kinsman Redeemer."

The MacArthur Bible Studies provide intriguing examinations of the whole of Scripture. Each guide incorporates extensive commentary, detailed observations on overriding themes, and probing questions to help you study the Word of God with guidance from John MacArthur.

ALSO AVAILABLE

In this study, John MacArthur guides readers through an in-depth look at this historical period beginning with the miraculous birth of Samuel, continuing through Saul's crowning as Israel's first king, and concluding with his tragic death. Studies include close-up examinations of Hannah, Eli, Saul, David, and Jonathan, as well as careful considerations of doctrinal themes such as "Slaying a Giant" and "Respecting God's Anointed."

The MacArthur Bible Studies provide intriguing examinations of the whole of Scripture. Each guide incorporates extensive commentary, detailed observations on overriding themes, and probing questions to help you study the Word of God with guidance from John MacArthur.

ALSO AVAILABLE

In this study, John MacArthur guides readers through an in-depth look at the historical period beginning with David's struggle to establish his throne, continuing through his sin and repentance, and concluding with the tragic rebellion of his son Absalom. Studies include close-up examinations of Joab, Amnon, Tamar, Absalom, and others, as well as careful considerations of doctrinal themes such as "Obedience and Blessing" and being a "Man After God's Own Heart."

The MacArthur Bible Studies provide intriguing examinations of the whole of Scripture. Each guide incorporates extensive commentary, detailed observations on overriding themes, and probing questions to help you study the Word of God with guidance from John MacArthur.